This book looks a very thorough
What makes Dr. Fape's study sp ____, valuable is his combination
of Biblical and African perspectives together with his personal
confidence in the decisive overthrow of the powers of darkness by
Christ at the Cross.

Dr. John R. W. Stott

POWERS IN ENCOUNTER
WITH POWER

*Paul's Concept of Spiritual Warfare
in Ephesians 6:10-12:
An African Christian Perspective*

M. Olusina Fape

MENTOR

ISBN 1 85792 873 3

Published in 2003
by
Christian Focus Publications
Geanies House, Fearn, Ross-shire,
IV20 1TW, Scotland

www.christianfocus.com

Cover design by Alister MacInnes

Printed and bound by
Bell & Bain Ltd, Glasgow

Contents

This book is dedicated to my wife

OLUWATOYIN KEHINDE FAPE

for her love and being a pillar of support to me in my ministry

Foreword

In a secular western culture the idea of Satan and spiritual warfare seems odd to many. We are so used to explaining things in terms of observable cause and effect. Even Christians can feel uncomfortable about New Testament teaching on this subject. So Paul's teaching about 'principalities and powers' has been reinterpreted to refer to political structures, and Satan has been described as a personification of the evil that stems from the human heart.

Writing from an African perspective, however, Michael Fape approaches the New Testament evidence in a wonderfully fresh way. He shows from his own culture how relevant this world view is. At the same time he wrestles carefully with the New Testament evidence to get a proper balance between the world, the flesh and the devil in Paul's theology.

Michael brings his scholarly ability to bear in the interpretation and application of the New Testament. He shows that the message of the cross and of Christ's resurrection and ascension has great power to defeat all the forces of evil in a culture where spiritual bondage is understood and acknowledged.

Michael's study of Acts and Ephesians shows how relevant the apostolic gospel would have been to the cultures where the gospel was first proclaimed. It is a reminder that any attempt to interpret those cultures in modern, secular terms is totally out of place. Moreover, Michael's review of the New Testament evidence in its historic context and in its application to modern African situations challenges our western view of the world and every attempt to remove the dimension of satanic power and spiritual warfare from our preaching and living.

Michael has thus contributed enormously not only to the Church in his own land but to Christian understanding more broadly as he has revisited this important New Testament topic. It has been a pleasure being involved with Michael in the fellowship of Oak Hill, as he has pursued this project.

Dr. David Peterson
Principal, Oak Hill College, London.

Acknowledgements

'Not unto us, O LORD, not unto us, but to Your name give glory because of Your mercy, and because of Your truth' (Ps. 115:1). Therefore, my first appreciation goes to the Lord God of heaven, who in His wisdom has bestowed on me the grace to undertake the research that has led to the publication of this book. To Him be the glory, dominion, power and majesty, forever and ever. Amen.

I am greatly indebted to the Langham Trust for awarding me the Langham Writers' Scholarship that has enabled me to undertake a year's postdoctoral studies at Oak Hill College, London, leading to the publication of this book. The financial assistance of this Trust cannot be quantified. I sincerely appreciate the extension of their generosity to my family by bringing them over to spend the last month with me in London.

My special thanks go to Dr. John Stott, the founder of the Langham Trust, and the initiator of the Langham Writers' Project, for his continued interest in developing sound evangelical scholars from the Third World. He is an asset to the kingdom of God in our generation. I thank him for finding the time to write to me personally, and also for arranging to meet me and share his thoughts with me in the course of the research. It is my prayer that the Lord will uphold him to the end of his Christian journey.

I am very grateful to Canon Paul Berg, the Administrator of the Langham Trust, who was directly in charge of this project. I appreciate all the various assistance rendered to ensure the success of my research work. I wish him God's continued blessing, sound health and renewed strength in His service.

The fact must be recognised that for a book of this nature to be successfully produced, there must be some unseen hands behind the scene. In this regard, I am greatly indebted to the following people: Dr. David Peterson, the Principal of Oak Hill College, London, and Dr. Chris Wright, International Ministry Director of the Langham Partnership. These scholars at different stages of the writing were responsible for reading through the manuscript of this book and offering many useful suggestions to improve the quality and style of writing. I also thank Dr. Peterson in a special way for writing the foreword to this book. Though these two scholars have made tremendous contributions to this work; nevertheless, since the book is mine, I take full responsibility for whatever imperfections that remain.

My gratitude goes to my father in the Lord, The Rt. Rev. G.I.O. Olajide (Retired Bishop of Ibadan), who recommended me for the Langham Writers' Scholarship at the eve of his retirement in January 2000. In spite of his tight schedule at that time, he still spared the time to put some quality words together to write a reference for me. Papa, thanks for your love and encouragement always. May the Lord spare your life and bless you with sound and robust health in your retirement.

In a similar way, I express profound thanks to my Bishop and his wife, The Rt. Rev. & Mrs J.O. Akinfenwa, who in my absence took exceptional care of my wife and children. Your words of encouragement throughout the period of my overseas trip contributed in a great measure to the successful completion of my research work and the subsequent publication of this book. It is my prayer that the good Lord will continue to watch over you and your family, and bless you with His wisdom to be able to shepherd His flock in Ibadan Diocese.

My appreciation goes to Dr. & Mrs Ade Abiodun and children, who made my short stay in London very enjoyable. I will forever cherish those moments we spent together in your home, first in London, and later in Luton. The hand of God will always be upon your family for good. To Eamon and Jean Brennan of Christ Church, Cockfosters, who provided a car for my use during the short visit of my family, I thank you for your love.

To the Congregation of All Souls' Parish Church, Bodija, Ibadan, I say a very big thank you. You are too many to mention individually. But God knows you all. I thank you for your spiritual, moral, and financial support. It is my prayer that God will continue to bless you all.

My profound gratitude goes to Mr. Malcolm Maclean of Christian Focus Publications and the entire staff of the organisation for the beautiful job done to ensure the publication of this book.

Last, but by no means least, my heartfelt and warm appreciation goes to my dear wife Toyin (to whom this book has been dedicated) and children, Moji, Sade, and Lola, for their love and understanding. I know that I have denied you the support and fellowship you would have loved to receive from me at some points while I was away. I could imagine your feelings in those moments of anxieties and fears. But in them all, the Lord was with you. The reality of the production of this book is a testimony to your readiness to put up with my inadequacies always. I sincerely appreciate your love. The Lord Jesus Christ will continue to strengthen our bond of love in Him.

While thanking you all, since we are all pilgrims here on earth who are involved in a day-to-day spiritual battle with the forces of darkness as we march on in the Christian journey, it is my earnest prayer that 'The God of peace will crush Satan under your feet shortly. Amen' (Rom. 16:20).

M.O.F.

Preface

Paul's concept of spiritual warfare in his epistles makes interesting reading if examined from an African Christian perspective. There is no other text that lends credence to this fact better than Ephesians 6:10-12. Many Bible scholars have interpreted a number of Paul's concepts in the abstract by depending more on contemporary social and political events, without bearing in mind the context of the language of the text and the prevailing cultural setting at the time it was written. This seems to be the case in relation to Paul's language of the *powers, principalities* and *spiritual warfare* in Ephesians 6:10-12.

It is not the intention of this study to cast aspersion on any previous work which tended to interpret Paul's language of the powers and principalities out of context due to the prevailing cultural gap. Rather, the main task of the study is to present a broader perspective of a significant Pauline concept within the appropriate context. As has been noted by O'Brien:

Any study of the principalities and powers quickly runs into problems of language, for the apostle Paul (not to mention other New Testament writers) uses terminology that is strange to us....The problem lies with many contemporary Western theologians and their cultural conditioning; they have allowed the latter to dictate their understanding of the biblical texts with the result that an increasingly fashionable view, viz., that the Pauline powers designate modern socio-political structures, has become the new orthodoxy.[1]

It is little wonder that many scholars, including Christians, have relegated the language of *the powers and principalities* to the realm of mere myth, which as a matter of necessity must be removed from Pauline theology, and not least Christian teaching. Dr. George Carey, the Archbishop of Canterbury, aptly notes this as he writes:

For some, such a picture is invalid because of its personalising of evil in the figure of Satan; it seems a crude, mythological concept with no right place in modern thought. Such debate can distract us from the essence of the image, which is that every Christian, and the Church as a whole, is in battle against the power of evil. Military theorists are aware that when it comes to battle you need to listen to your front-line troops because they are actually engaged with the enemy. So, with respect to the Church, we need to listen carefully not only to our philosophers and theologians in their exploration of modes of thought, but to the testimony of those who live on the frontiers of the world, in direct encounter with evil which echoes the teaching of Scriptures. So, even allowing for the fact that our world-view is necessarily different from that of the New Testament, we should not lightly devalue the Bible's pictures of the realities after which we are grasping.[2]

In actual fact, some thought that the idea of *forces of darkness* in the context of spiritual warfare was a mere myth which must not be linked to Paul, and of course must not be interpreted against the backdrop of the Scriptures. The reason according to Macgregor is that 'the scientific mind, preoccupied as it is with the observed sequences of physical cause and effect, rejects spiritualistic causality in every shape and form, and finds Paul's conception of "principalities and powers" controlling the destiny of man utterly alien and fantastic'.[3] That is why it is difficult today for the modern man to see the operation of the forces of darkness behind the fast disintegrating family structure, in the rise in the waves of crimes, and in perhaps a greater inclination towards the perversion of sexual orientation.

However, a re-reading of this passage from the viewpoint of an African Christian in the contextual cultural understanding of Acts 19:1-20 makes Paul's concept of spiritual warfare in Ephesians 6:10-12 less problematic. It brings out the reality of the forces of darkness in constant operation, seeking to frustrate the plan of God for mankind. The preference for an African interpretation is informed by the operations of the principalities and powers in the African culture, a situation that makes the preaching of the gospel very attractive to the Africans, as a means of liberating them from the powers of darkness. This needs to be emphasised in order to align the present study with the view of the contemporary western theologians who often argue that biblical texts, for example the ones on slavery and women as found in Luke 4:18 and Galatians 3:27-29, must be read in recognition of the present social struggle. The essence of such a move is to de-ideologise traditional western scholarship.

While our effort in this work is not to advance any liberation theology from a political point of view, yet it is our aim to probe Ephesians 6:10-12 from the perspective of African socio-cultural world, looking for a meaningful interpretation. As we undertake this study, our task is to attempt a re-reading of our selected text with a view to making it relevant to an African mind. What are the implications of this text for African Christians in the contemporary church? Howard Marshall's view that the study of the New Testament cannot be limited to the original recipients without thinking of its relevance to contemporary society is appropriate here as we attempt to contextualise this study. As he correctly writes:

> New Testament interpretation is not concerned solely to lay bare the meaning of the text for its original readers but reaches its goal only when it examines the meaning of the text for today and allows the text to affect our own attitudes and understanding.[4]

The purpose of this study, therefore, is to explain the gospel as the power of God for salvation (to use Paul's own language in Romans 1:16), as we look at 'powers' in Ephesians 6:10-12 from the understanding of an African as weapons for defence in the face of the vicissitudes and dangers of life. Therefore if Paul's message of salvation is to have any relevance to an African mind, it must be read within the framework of contextual understanding of the operations of the principalities and powers as a matter of spiritual warfare, from which the power of God is the only solution.

There are nine chapters in this book. Chapter 1 looks at the origins of the principalities and powers, and for the onset of spiritual warfare. In a way, the chapter prepares the ground for the rest of our discussion in the subsequent chapters. Chapters 2-5 attempt to look at Paul's distinctive language of the principalities and powers in Ephesians 6:10-12, in the light of his mission strategy in the book of the Acts. The main task here is to show that Paul's use of the language of the principalities and powers in Ephesians 6:10-12 in particular, and the rest of his epistles in general, is informed by his experience on the mission field.

Furthermore, this section reveals that, while some human institutions may be working at variance with the proclamation of the good news, Paul does not see these human institutions as being inherently evil, except in the operations of the kingdom of darkness behind them manifesting its powers in the concrete actions of human agents. In the view of Paul, the irony of the victory of Christ lies in His crucifixion by the powers of darkness. While the powers of darkness thought they were terminating the ministry of Christ by crucifying Him, unknown to them they were in actual fact executing eternal judgement of defeat on their own kingdom.

Chapter 6 focuses on the African concept of spiritual warfare and examines the various weapons for fighting the same. To further our discussion in this chapter, a few probing questions will be asked. Why are the Africans taking refuge in these forces of darkness as a means of safety? How futile is it to do so? What becomes of the powers of darkness in their face-to-face encounter with the Power of God, who is Jesus Christ (1 Cor. 1:24)? Is there any affinity between the socio-cultural settings of the city of Ephesus of Paul's day and the African society of our contemporary milieu with regard to the operations of the powers of darkness?

Chapters 7 and 8, the climax of this study, demonstrate the powerlessness of the forces of darkness, that is, the powers and principalities in their face-to-face encounter with 'the Power of God' – Jesus Christ (1 Cor. 1:24). Specifically here, Christ is presented as the deliverer from the stronghold of the powers of darkness. This section also draws attention to the fact that though in Christ the forces of darkness have been defeated and believers have been set free, yet there is the need for believers to be on their guard by putting on 'the whole armour of God' in their journey of faith.

In chapter 9, which concludes the book, an attempt is made to demonstrate that the victory of believers over the powers of darkness is a call for service in their new dispensation of liberty. By being in the service of the Lord, believers will ensure the permanence of their victory here and now as they also await the final defeat of the forces of darkness at the second coming of Christ.

This book should not be seen as a mere theological treatise. The purpose, as stated earlier, is that readers would appreciate the salvation message contained in Ephesians 6:10-12 in a greater dimension as God's power to rescue humanity from the operation of the forces of darkness, which are a reality to an African mind. More importantly it is composed to expose believers of all races and cultures to the fact that forces of darkness are at work in our own generation, and to inform them of the need to measure up to the challenges coming from the kingdom of darkness by way of spiritual warfare. Therefore, believers should be acquainted with the nature of this spiritual warfare, and the resources at their disposal to fight the battle of faith in the light of the events of the death and resurrection of Christ. In other words, this study seeks to demonstrate the fact that the victory of Christ over the *powers* of darkness, as signalled in His death and resurrection, also means *victory* and *power* for believers over 'the powers and principalities' in all situations.

It is my prayer that every reader of this book will be encouraged by its contents to find strength to face the challenges from the world as we continue our pilgrimage with a view to overcoming the powers of darkness that may want to cause any obstacle as we run the race that is set before us.

1

A Biblical Account of the Origins of the Powers and Spiritual Warfare

Introduction

Powers? Probably the first task that should be addressed as we seek to approach our subject is to get a clear understanding of what we mean by the word *powers*. By seeking to discuss the subject of *power*, we are not attempting either to probe into the realms of political philosophy or social ethics. Instead, what we are simply trying to do is 'to reconstruct [within the realm of biblical studies] something of the world of thought in which Paul's mind was at home'.[1]

Therefore, our use of *powers* is without any political undertone in the sense of the exercise of authority depicting the *ruler* and the *ruled* in a civil context. The term *powers* will be understood in the context of spiritual forces operating in the *kingdom of darkness* and attempting to frustrate the plan of God for mankind. In other words, we shall be using this term within the framework of *spiritual entities in direct opposition to the divine rule of God*. As we seek to do this, our discussion shall be undertaken from three perspectives, in each case seeking to explore the origins of Satan, the powers and spiritual warfare.

Towards the origins of Satan

What can we know about the origin of this invisible being from the pages of Scripture? Are there explicit references to his creation? All that we know from Genesis 1 and 2 is the simple and yet orderly account of the 'creation of the heavens and earth' (Gen. 1:1), and subsequently the creation of inanimate objects and animate creatures – including mankind (Gen. 1:3-31; 2:4-24).

A creature appears in Genesis 3, the serpent, which the earlier account did not mention. Is this a matter of oversight? At first, this may look like a riddle. We must, therefore, look more carefully into Scripture, if we would find explanations of the origin of the serpent, who is known in other texts of the Bible by names such as Satan, Devil, Lucifer or the Dragon.[2]

Three Old Testament books mention the name 'Satan', namely Job, 1 Chronicles and Zechariah. In Job, Satan is mentioned in the opening chapters where his role is primarily that of an accuser. He is pictured as on the look out for possible reasons for accusing those operating in the will of God. If Satan finds any human beings sinning against God (Job 1:6-12; 2:1-7), he can quickly bring up a charge against them before God. In 1 Chronicles 21:1, Satan 'stood up against Israel, and moved the heart of David to number Israel'. Again, the function of Satan is that of an adversary, moving the heart of David to act contrary to the will of God. In Zechariah 3:1-2, Satan stood to oppose Joshua, the high priest. In these three instances, Satan functioned in the capacity of an adversary, trying to oppose man, or preventing him from operating in accordance with the will of God.

While these passages may seem to be the only explicit references to Satan in the Old Testament, there appears to be a much earlier implicit mention of the same creature in Genesis 3, where he is referred to as the serpent:

> 'Now the serpent was more cunning than any beast of the field which the Lord God had made. And he said to the woman, 'Has God indeed said, "You shall not eat of every tree of the garden"?' And the serpent said to the woman, 'You will not surely die. For God knows that in the day you eat of it your eyes will be opened, and you will be like God, knowing good and evil' (Gen. 3:1, 4-5).

The role performed in the Garden of Eden is very much the same as that of the accuser in the passages where 'Satan' is mentioned explicitly.

The fact that the name *Satan* was not used in Genesis 3:1, 4-5, does not alter his real identity as a being created by God. For we read in Colossians 1:16:, 'For by Him all things were created that are in heaven and that are on earth, visible and invisible, whether thrones or dominions or principalities or powers. All things were created through Him and for Him.'

According to Psalm 8:5a, man 'was made a little lower than the angels'. To say that God created the angels for specific purposes is not a mere speculation. The Bible bears witness to this fact. The first reason for which the angels were created is to worship God. Hence the Scripture says, 'Let all the angels of God worship Him' (Heb. 1:6b).

Secondly, the angels were created as ministering spirits. 'But to which of the angels has He ever said: "Sit at My right hand, till I make Your enemies Your footstool?" Are they not all ministering spirits sent forth to minister for those who will inherit salvation?' (Heb. 1:13-14). The angels have a noble task as 'ministering spirits sent forth to minister to those who will inherit salvation' (Heb. 1:14). Examples abound, both in the Old and New Testaments, of where the angels ministered to humans (Gen. 16:7-12; Dan. 10:10-21; Matt. 1:20-25; Luke 1:11-17).

For the angels to be able to worship and serve God in His presence, they must have been created holy, with great perfection. As Timmons writes, 'angels were created with great strength, wisdom, and beauty. Their main purpose was to help God administer His government and kingdom throughout the universe.'[3] While we concur with Timmons' opinion on the 'strength', 'wisdom' and 'beauty' of the angels, his claim that they were created 'to help God administer His government and kingdom' leaves much to be desired. God is the sole administrator of the universe, and He does not require the assistance of any creature to administer it. But if Timmons' view is from the perspective of 'ministering angels', invisible spiritual beings in regular service of God being sent on errands, then the ambiguity is removed.

In the creation of the angelic beings, there is a clear indication that the creation of Satan was of particular uniqueness. This can be inferred from the text in Ezekiel 28:12b-14:

You were the seal of perfection, full of wisdom and perfect in beauty. You were in Eden, the garden of God; every precious stone was your covering; the sardis, topaz, and diamond, Beryl, onyx, and jasper, Sapphire, turquoise, and emerald with gold. The workmanship of your timbrels and pipes was prepared for you on the day you were created. You were the anointed cherub who covers; I established you;

you were on the holy mountain of God; you walked back and forth in the midst of fiery stones.[4]

But where is the mention of Satan in this passage? By seeing a Satan-Lucifer figure in this passage, are we not trying to import a strange idea into this text, which the author of Ezekiel might not have intended? For our immediate purpose, there are three points to help us identify the feature of a Satan-character here. First, there is the mention of an 'anointed cherub'. A cherub[5] is an angelic being, regularly in the service of God. Simply put, a cherub is a ministering angel (Gen. 3:24, Ezek. 1:5-14; 10:9-16). An 'anointed cherub' in this sense would be understood as *a cherub among many cherubim, marked out for higher services*. To 'be anointed' is to be set apart by God for a special assignment. In the Old Testament, kings were anointed for leadership roles (1 Sam. 10:1; 2 Sam. 2:4). Also, in the New Testament, Christ was anointed specifically for the redemption of mankind (Luke 4:18-19; Acts 10:38). Understood from this perspective, Satan, as 'an anointed cherub', must have been set apart by God for a special purpose at his creation. If juxtaposed with the text in Isaiah 14 (which will receive attention below), it would seem as if this special feature was the backdrop to Satan's pride.

Secondly, the mention of the presence of the anointed cherub in the Garden of Eden would, by implication, mean that Satan (an 'anointed cherub') was in the garden of God before his fall, and ultimately before the fall of man. The Garden of Eden here could mean the abode of God, since God is depicted as 'walking in the garden in the cool of the day' (Gen. 3:8), where He was in regular contact with Adam and Eve before the fall.

Thirdly, there is the mention of the walking 'back and forth' in Ezekiel 28:14.[6] Again, another passage of Scripture sheds more light on the identity of the personality involved here. In Job 1, Satan is seen manifesting the same disposition as contained in Ezekiel 28:14. 'And the LORD said to Satan, "From where do you come?" So Satan answered the LORD and said, "From going to and fro on the earth, and from walking back and forth on it" ' (Job 1:7). The response of Satan in Job chapter one is an indication of the fact that even after his fall, he still continues to manifest his character of 'walking to and fro', 'like a roaring lion seeking whom he may devour' (1 Pet. 5:8).

From the foregoing, it is our contention that God created Satan originally as an angelic being, an 'anointed cherub' with the privilege of serving in the presence of God. This great privilege of service gave him the benefit of being 'in Eden, the Garden of God', where he was expected to serve God in obedience. Thus Satan is a creature, whose creation perhaps predated that of mankind.

Towards the origins of powers
God does not keep us in the dark as to the origin of the beginning of the unending conflict between His own Kingdom and the kingdom of Darkness. The Scripture gives an accurate account of this rebellion, the beginning of the conflict, and the origin of the powers and principalities. There are three accounts, two in the Old Testament and one in the New Testament. First, we will consider the account in the book of the prophet Isaiah:

> How you are fallen from heaven, O Lucifer, son of the morning! How you are cut down to the ground, who weakened the nations! For you have said in your heart: 'I will ascend into heaven, I will exalt my throne above the stars of God; I will also sit on the mount of the congregation on the farthest sides of the north; I will ascend above the heights of the clouds, I will be like the Most High.' You shall be brought down to Sheol, to the lowest depths of the Pit (Isa.14:12-15).

One statement that comes to mind in connection with this text is that of Jesus in Luke 10:18: 'I saw Satan fall like lightning from heaven.' This was in response to the joyful reports of the *seventy* sent out on a mission trip, who claimed in the preceding verse that 'even demons are subject to us in Your [Jesus] name' (10:17). Could it be that Jesus was calling to remembrance the calamity that had already befallen Satan when he rebelled against God, and was demoted from his position of honour? Or was Jesus making a prophetic statement about what would happen to Satan at the end of the age? Whichever way, one point comes out clearly, and this is the fact that in the present world, Satan has been stripped of his power in the arrival of Christ (Luke 11:20). In the view of Ladd,

'This again is obviously symbolic language asserting that the presence of the power of the Kingdom of God on earth in the person of Jesus and his disciples meant the toppling of Satan from his place of power.'[7] Therefore in the meantime, the final doom of Satan is expected at the second coming of Christ, when his power will be lost forever.[8]

However, Isaiah 14 has generated a lot of scholarly discussion and has been interpreted metaphorically by some scholars who suggest that it should not be regarded as relevant for determining the origin of the fall of Satan. For instance, Calvin writes:

> The exposition of this passage, which some have given, as if it referred to Satan, has arisen from ignorance; for the context plainly shows that these statements must be understood in reference to the king of the Babylonians. But when passages of Scripture are taken up at random, and no attention is paid to the context, we need not wonder that mistakes of this kind frequently arise. Yet it was an instance of very gross ignorance, to imagine that Lucifer was the king of devils, and that the Prophet gave him this name.[9]

Oswalt, following in the footsteps of Calvin, also does not see the text as a basis for explaining the fall of Satan. For him, the passage is an attempt to explain the pride of a human king, a tradition that was prevalent among the Canaanites. Hence he writes:

> Some of the church fathers, linking this passage to Luke 10:18 and Revelation 12:8, 9, took it to refer to the fall of Satan described in those places. However, the great expositors of the Reformation were unanimous in arguing that the context here does not support such an interpretation.[10]

While Calvin and others might rejected interpreting Isaiah 14:12-16 as depicting the fall of Satan, some church fathers, such as Jerome and Tertullian, believed the text was a reference to the fall of Satan. Ridderbos concurs with the views of these church fathers when he writes:

> Still, there is an element of truth in the idea: by his self-deification Babylon's king is the imitator of the devil and the type of the Antichrist

(Dan. 11:36; 2 Thess. 2:4); therefore his humiliation also is an example of Satan's fall from the position of power that he has usurped (cf. Luke 10:18; Rev. 12:9). Thus he who had such high aspiration is now deeply humbled.[11]

Even if we agree that the reference above is not to be taken literally as applying to Lucifer, yet the prophet must have borrowed his metaphor from an event of great historical reliability. According to John Watts, who sees in the passage an element of poetry, 'When the poem has been used in apocryphal and Christian circles to picture the fall of an angelic Satan, the reference must be to the shadowy mythical background of the poem rather than to the poem itself.'[12] Granted that Isaiah 14 is a poem, yet in the view of Wildberger:

> The poem obviously contains material that has been reworked, using mythological ideas originating among non-Israelite peoples; and, since the Ugaritic texts were discovered, it has become clear that these myths came to be known in Israel via the Canaanites. The parallel texts in the book of Ezekiel have reworked extensively the same mythological material....There must have been a tradition in Israel, which had been reworked and reworked many times, according to which the pride and downfall of foreign rulers was depicted by using graphic portrayals that originated in heathen myths.[13]

It is clear from Isaiah 14:12-14 that what occasioned the fall of Lucifer was his pride. What Lucifer wanted was a position that was higher than that of his Creator. This is pride of the highest order. While Lucifer thought of raising his status above that of the Most High, what he actually got was a demotion of status, since his action led to his being 'brought down to Sheol [and] to the lowest depths of the Pit.'

In other words, Isaiah did not develop his idea in a vacuum; rather he has likened the fall of the king of Babylonia to the fall of Satan, an event that took place at a particular point in time. Therefore, for our purpose here, the passage does offer some revelation about the fall of Satan.

Another account is contained in the book of Ezekiel. While there is explicit reference to Lucifer in the text from Isaiah, such is absent from Ezekiel.[14] Yet there are similarities between the two passages, which suggest that Ezekiel must have used a tradition similar to the one used by Isaiah. Ezekiel writes:

> You were perfect in your ways from the day you were created, till iniquity was found in you....Your heart was lifted up because of your beauty; you corrupted your wisdom for the sake of your splendour, I cast you to the ground....All who knew you among the peoples are astonished at you; you have become a horror, and shall be no more forever [to minister before me] (28:15, 17, 19).

From the time of the early church fathers, the reference to the king of Tyre has been seen as having been portrayed in terms of the fall of Lucifer. Thus Block writes:

> During the second temple period, the view developed that Ezek. 28 was based on a tradition of an angelic 'fall,' closely associated with the 'fall' of humanity. Since the time of Origen many conservative Christians in particular have equated the king of Tyre with Lucifer (= Satan), 'Brilliant One, son of the morning,'...mentioned in Isa. 14:12. Accordingly, Ezekiel's prophecy is thought to recount the circumstances of the original fall of Satan, who had previously been one of the cherubim attending the throne of God.[15]

The interpretation that the above passage has relevance to the original status of Satan and his fall has the support of Unger, who writes: 'One passage, Ezekiel 28:11-19, despite contention to the contrary, obviously transcends reference to the "prince of Tyre," or to Adam in Eden, and embraces a splendid and detailed portrait of Satan's person in his primeval sinless glory.'[16] We need to pay more attention to the language of Ezekiel. Verse 15 is highly significant: 'You were perfect in your ways from the day you were created, till iniquity was found in you.' The language of this verse would make the reference highly inappropriate to any mortal king. It is our contention that the passage serves two purposes. First, it explains the original nature of Satan before his fall, and secondly, it shows his condition after his fall.

In Ezekiel 28, pride was the occasion for the rebellion of Lucifer.

The basis for boasting was his beauty and wisdom. Satan had forgotten that these two special attributes, for which his heart was lifted up, were from God. The consequence of this action also brought about Satan's expulsion from the presence of God, since he was 'cast…to the ground'. In other words, God is the Lord over *all*. Nothing can violate His omnipotence. Ordinary creatures, no matter how affluent, brilliant, beautiful or advanced (to use the modern day information technology language) can query or challenge His authority. He is the *all-in-all*.

If the earlier two accounts have left the readers of this work in doubt as to the correctness of our proposition, that is, our attempt to establish the origin of the *powers* (which we are seeking to trace directly to the fall of Satan), the third account in the New Testament as contained in the book of Revelation helps to remove this obscurity:

> And war broke out in heaven: Michael and his angels fought against the dragon; and the dragon and his angels fought, but they did not prevail, nor was a place found for them in heaven any longer. So the great dragon was cast out, that serpent of old, called the Devil, and Satan, who deceives the whole world; he was cast to the earth, and his angels were cast out with him (Rev. 12:7-9).

While it is our contention that Revelation 12 plays a significant role in explaining the fall of Satan, and the subsequent spiritual warfare between the Kingdom of God and kingdom of darkness, there are some scholars who differ from this view. For instance, Mounce says that the text 'does not refer to the original expulsion of Satan from heaven'.[17] However, from the viewpoint of David Aune, this text, when viewed from the Jewish mythological perspective, fits in as the real explanation for the fall of Satan:

> Since the combat myths in which the hero fights a dragon regularly end with the destruction of the dragon, this variant has been adapted to the primeval Jewish myth of the fall of Satan. The myth of the heavenly battle between Michael and Satan resulting in the defeat and expulsion of Satan and his angels from heaven (vv 7-9) is narrated as an eschatological event in 12:9 as it is in Luke 10:18.[18]

A note of caution is necessary here. While any reader may be tempted to read this passage eschatologically, as a matter of an event that is merely anticipated in the future, yet its language makes it clear that it refers to an action that has already been concluded, though it still has serious implications for the final victory to be won over the powers of darkness at the second coming of Christ. The view of Ladd is helpful here:

> Theologically, the clue to this battle is given in vs. 11: 'And they have conquered him by the blood of the Lamb.' In redemptive history the victory over Satan was won by Christ through the shedding of his blood on the cross. We have no other scriptural support for the idea that the achievement of redemption, which included the overthrow and the final defeat of evil, is the work of angels; it is altogether the work of Christ.[19]

Revelation 12:7-12 is very significant for our present discussion in that it sheds great light on the origin of the *powers* and *principalities*. There are a few points to be noted in this text. By considering these points carefully, they will further help us to establish in a reasonable way the origin of the *powers* and *principalities* from the New Testament point of view as will be seen later in chapters 3–5.

Firstly, the different names given to Satan in the various texts of Scripture find their point of convergence here. The above text reveals Satan in all his true identities, as the 'dragon', 'serpent of old', 'the devil', and 'the deceiver'. The dragon is seen as the old serpent, who visited Adam and Eve in the Garden of Eden, and caused their fall (Gen. 3:1-7). Indeed, Satan is a deceiver who, in the words of Paul, comes to lead men astray from the way of truth, 'But I fear, lest somehow, as the serpent deceived Eve by his craftiness, so your minds may be corrupted from the simplicity that is in Christ' (2 Cor. 11:3). He is the devil, who walks about roaring like a lion seeking whom to devour (1 Pet 5:8).

Secondly, in God's original plan of creation Satan was 'in heaven', since the war that led to his expulsion was fought in heaven. It was his expulsion that made him a fallen angel, having been 'cast out' of heaven. This would then mean that prior to his fall, he occupied a unique position of honour and excellence. This accounted for the singular privilege given to him to worship God and serve before Him continually as one of the angels (Heb. 1:6).

Thirdly, while there is no clear indication as to what led to the war in heaven between Michael and the dragon,[20] by viewing this passage against the backdrop of Isaiah 14, it could be postulated that Satan was not satisfied with the position assigned to him by God as a chief ministering angel. This was responsible for his desire to establish his own throne above the throne of the 'Most High', wanting to be on a par with Him (Isa. 14:14).

Fourthly, God will not share His glory with any creature, no matter how excellent its nature. This accounted for the expulsion, or the 'casting out' of Satan from the presence of God. Specifically, he was dispossessed of his right to live in the Garden of Eden (Ezek. 28:12).

Fifthly, it is conjectured that Satan did not readily accept the sentence of God upon his life. As a result he masterminded a rebellion against God, and consequently a war broke out in heaven to demonstrate his opposition to the authority of God (Rev. 12:7).

Sixthly, not only did Satan oppose God, but also at the same time he succeeded in recruiting some angelic beings by instigating them to rebel against God. Undoubtedly, these were 'the angels who did not keep their proper domain, but left their own habitation' (Jude 6 cf. 2 Pet. 2:4). In other words, Satan created a rebellious *kingdom* for himself, which he himself headed. The fact of the existence of such a kingdom was alluded to both by the Pharisees and Jesus Christ. 'Now when the Pharisees heard it they said, "This fellow [Christ] does not cast out demons except by Beelzebub, the ruler of the demons." But Jesus said to them, "If Satan casts out Satan, he is divided against himself. How then will his kingdom stand?" ' (Matt. 12:24-26).

The fact that there was a 'ruler' in the hierarchy of the powers of darkness presupposes a kingdom. In this kingdom were Satan (the ruler) and his angels who were 'cast out with him' at the outbreak of war in heaven (Rev. 12:9). In other words, the biblical fact is that Satan and his cohorts were created sinless at the beginning to serve and worship God. But on account of their rebellion, they were expelled from the presence of God. This was the inauguration of the *kingdom of darkness*, and invariably the subsequent emergence of *the powers and principalities*.

The powers and principalities therefore, can be simply defined as *fallen angels who have been expelled from the presence of God, but who are now in direct spiritual confrontation with the Kingdom of God*.[21] This will adequately explain one of the titles of Satan as the 'devil', which means 'the chief opponent of God'.[22] What Satan seeks to do right from the time of his expulsion from the presence of God is to keep recruiting the legions of his army from among mankind to oppose anything that is godly. Thus, according to O'Brien, 'The principalities and powers can be understood as personal, supernatural intelligences, emissaries of the god of this world, which seek to influence the world and mankind for ill at every level, using every resource at their disposal.'[23] In other words, powers and principalities are all subordinate to Satan. Again, O'Brien writes:

> One distinction, however, is clearly drawn in the New Testament, viz. that the demons, spirits, angels, principalities and powers are regarded as subordinate to Satan or the devil. They are his innumerable powers seen as organised into a single empire (note especially Mark 3:22-30; cf. Luke 10:17f.; Rev. 12:9; 16:13ff.). They are manifestations of the devil's power.[24]

In the light of the above it is clear that the kingdom of darkness has an organisational structure, the head of which is Satan. In co-operation with Satan are the powers and principalities, rulers of the darkness of this age, and spiritual hosts of wickedness in the heavenly places. These are the spiritual entities who are always fighting tooth and nail in the ongoing spiritual warfare in the present world. These forces of darkness are always contending with God in respect of His absolute ownership of the whole universe, and especially His right to demand absolute obedience from human beings created after His own image. Thus, what Satan aims at doing is to cause man equally to rebel against God through disobedience.

Towards the origin of spiritual warfare

Having considered the origin of the powers and principalities, it is important at this juncture that we take look into the origin of *spiritual warfare*. Once again the passage in the book of Revelation is very helpful:

> And war broke out in heaven: Michael and his angels fought against the dragon; and the dragon and his angels fought, but they did not prevail, nor was a place found for them in heaven any longer. So the great dragon was cast out, that serpent of old, called the Devil, and Satan, who deceives the whole world; he was cast to the earth, and his angels were cast out with him (Rev. 12:7-9).

Although the eschatological implications of the above passage are not to be ruled out, for our immediate purpose we shall be concerned solely with how it offers explanation for the origin of spiritual warfare, a matter of the ongoing conflict between the Kingdom of God and kingdom of darkness.

While it is true that the main plan of Satan is to oppose the kingly rule of God by fighting against His kingdom continually, it is humanity that Satan has made the punch bag. It is absolutely impossible for Satan to defeat God. What he can do is to try to frustrate the plan of God, and the most obvious way he chooses to do this is by attacking human beings. In other words, spiritual *warfare is Satan's projection of the anger of his defeat by God to man (created by God, as the crown of His work of creation) in order to prevent man for enjoying full fellowship with God.* This explains his real identity as Satan, 'the adversary and accuser of the brethren.'

The creation of man was to show forth the beauty and glory of God, and to provide in his offspring worthy servants for God. Man at his creation was given unlimited dominion over every other thing created by God, including angels (Gen. 1:28). This is to be understood in the fact that at the end of the age, man has been vested with the authority even to judge the angels (1 Cor. 6:3). Satan and his cohorts, knowing fully that they have lost the battle to rise above the 'Most High', now shift their attention to man, who has been described as 'the crown of God's work of creation'.[25]

Simply put, Satan knows that man has been created for something special, and is very dear to the heart of God. The implication of this is that man has authority over Satan, since on account of his fall he has been demoted and sent to the earth.

Therefore what he seeks to do is to frustrate this excellent plan of God for humanity. The fact that Satan has been sent to the planet earth should not pose any problem. The appearance of the serpent in the garden later shows that immediately after his expulsion from heaven he quickly assumed the role of an accuser; and 'like a roaring lion he seeks whom he may devour' (1 Pet. 5:8). In other words, Satan does not want man to rule over him. Herein lies the record of the first warfare on earth. This warfare became evident in the visit of Satan, 'the serpent of old' who employed his cunning wiles to exercise control over humanity by corrupting the will of our first parents in the Garden of Eden.

The main intention of Satan was to cause man to disobey God. The method he adopted was cleverly to trick man to believing that he could be made wise as God, and of course to make man see God as selfish. He wanted to make man believe that God was unfair to him. This informed the appearance of Satan as he posed himself as an advocate:

> And he [the serpent] said to the woman, 'Has God indeed said you shall not eat of every tree of the garden.' And the woman said to the serpent, 'We may eat the fruit of the trees of the garden; but of the fruit of the tree which is in the midst of the garden, God has said, "You shall not eat it, nor shall you touch it, lest you die." ' And the serpent said to the woman, 'You shall not surely die. For God knows that in the day you eat of it your eye will be opened, and you will be like God, knowing good and evil' (Gen. 3:1, 4-5).

Both Satan and Eve lied against God by completely misrepresenting Him. First, God did not say, as in the erronious accusation of Satan, that Adam and Eve should 'not eat of every tree of the garden'. Secondly, neither did God say, as in the words of Eve, that they should not 'touch it'. How soon was Eve to forget the words of God! She did not keep God's words in her heart, and this was responsible for her sinning against God. At any rate, Satan had no right to say man would not die! Man did die (Prov. 14:12). This is why Jesus Christ calls him 'the father of lies' (John 8:44). Certainly, Satan had a hidden agenda for man. He only wanted to prevent man from remaining in this privileged position with God. He did not want humanity to take over the glory and position of honour that had been removed from him. However, it should be noted that we are not suggesting that the fall of Satan is coordinate with the fall of man. While in His mercy God made provision to redeem man from his fallen state, Satan is not privileged to such a redemptive plan.

The fact that the serpent was able to engage in dialogue with Adam and Eve in the Garden of Eden revealed a unique aspect of his creation. This was an indication that his existence predated that of man. This brief, but disastrous encounter of Satan with man was a reflection of the vestiges of his original privileged position. Of course, he used this singular advantage to lure mankind from his position of excellence. Stressing the importance of Satan's speech as a revelation of the fact of his creation before man, Page writes:

> Of greater interest and significance than the serpent's ability to talk is what the animal says. He reveals preternatural knowledge, beginning with his first words to Eve, 'Did God really say, "You must not eat from any tree in the garden"?' (Gen. 3:1). How does the serpent know about the prohibition against eating the forbidden fruit? Not only is his knowledge of the prohibition unexpected, but also he implies that he knows more about the fruit than God has revealed.[27]

Without any doubt, Satan had free access to the throne of God before his fall. He was a creature greatly honoured by God. This was the advantage Satan had over Adam and Eve and he maximised it to alter the destiny of human beings, until the arrival of the Seed of the woman who came to deliver humanity from the bondage of Satan (1 Tim. 2:15). It is true that man did not immediately die physically by violating the divine command of God, yet it marked the beginning of his spiritual death, and ultimately his physical death.

Yes, man was in a face-to-face encounter with the powers from the kingdom of darkness in the first-ever recorded spiritual warfare in the Bible. Man had already received a command from God, who loved him and committed the pleasure of the Garden of Eden to him. Only 'of the tree of the knowledge of good and evil you shall not eat, for in the day that you eat of it you shall surely die' (Gen. 2:17).

Satan, the archenemy of God who is waging a serious battle with God in respect of His authority, now came to confront man with a suggestion that seems better to man than the command he had received from God.[28] Man was torn between two opinions, or rather let us say between two choices. He was confronted with the choice of whether to obey God, his Creator or to obey the fallen angel, who unknowingly to man is just trying 'to steal [his authority and pleasure], kill and destroy' him (John 10:10a). Man chose to obey the enemy of God. This is the fall of man, the beginning of misery and agonising experience for humanity.

Man has disobeyed God, and Satan has consequently achieved his goal of preventing man from taking over his exalted position in the plan of God from which he had been expelled. Whatever remains therefore is a matter of *spiritual warfare* for man, an ongoing lifetime struggle; the choice of who to obey – God or Satan, to do good or evil? In other words, there is no cessation in this battle until the Parousia, when Christ returns in His glory at the close of the age. That is when Satan and the principalities and powers will be consigned to their eternal home in hell. The view of Archbishop Carey lends credence to our discussion as he describes the end of the warfare between the Kingdom of God and kingdom of darkness as he sees the final abode of Satan, the principalities and powers in hell:

> A third image [of hell] is of the end of the battle between good and evil, between God and the epitome of the powers of evil named in Scriptures as 'Satan' or the Devil. Pictures of this can be seen in many early Christian frescoes, from the third century onwards. The world is a battleground between two forces, in an unrelenting fight which will only end when Christ returns in glory, and the promise of his kingdom of justice and love is fulfilled. Then, in [the] Scripture image, will come the judgement, when Satan and all the forces of evil will be judged and sentenced, and banished to hell.[28]

While it is certain that the final dooms day awaits the forces of darkness at the return of Christ, when they will be banished to hell, until then humanity is involved in this life-long battle. This battle of whom to obey in the present existence could possibly be the backdrop against which we might understand the plight of man as echoed by Paul in Romans 7:18-19, 22-24:

> For I know that in me (that is, in my flesh) nothing good dwells; for to will is present with me, but how to perform what is good I do not find. For the good that I will to do, I do not do; but the evil I will not to do, that I practice.... For I delight in the law of God according to the inward man. But I see another law in my members, warring against the law of my mind, and bringing me into captivity to the law of sin which is in my members. O wretched man that I am! Who will deliver me from this body of death?

Spiritual warfare is a matter of harnessing all resources at ones disposal for the purpose of bringing another person into a position of subjection. In other words, spiritual warfare involves exertion of positional influence to exercise illegitimate authority over other individuals for negative results. This is exactly what Satan always does, using his positional influence of his intimate knowledge of God and His word (Matt. 4:6) to trick man by making him disobey God so as to prevent him from finding fulfilment in Him.

However, in the cross of Christ God has once again stripped Satan of his power over mankind, making it possible for humanity to have sweet fellowship with Him. It in this connection that Green writes:

> Jesus knows that the devil has usurped God's place of leadership in this world: it does lie in his hand to bestow 'all the kingdoms of the world and the glory of them' (Matt. 4:8), and Jesus does not deny it. But rather than compromise with this subtle and evil force, Jesus knows that he must oppose him to the bitter end. Hence the way of the cross. That was to sound the death knell for the usurper prince of this age. It was as he spoke of the cross that Jesus cried, 'Now is the judgement of this world. Now shall the ruler of this world be cast out. And I, when I am lifted up from the earth, will draw all men to myself' (John 12:31f).[29]

Though Satan has arrogated to himself all that belongs to God by causing man to disobey in the Garden of Eden, yet in the Cross of Christ he met his complete failure.[30] Satan is now defeated and dispossessed of his vaunted power. In anger at his defeat, Satan is merely left to roar 'like a lion' (1 Pet. 5:8), because Christ is 'the only Lion of the tribe of Judah' (Rev. 5:5).

Conclusion

At this point we will give a brief overview. So far, what we have tried to do is to establish three points. First, we have offered an explanation for the origin of Satan. In other words, Satan was, and is still, a creature, beautifully created by God and given the privilege of service in the Garden of Eden. However, because of his inherent beauty, he was filled with pride and sought to exalt his position above that of the Most High. Such a thought led to his fall from the privileged position given to him by God, and he was consequently driven out of the Garden of God.

Secondly, we have offered an explanation for the origin of the *powers*. We have suggested that *powers* should be understood in the context of *Satan and the fallen angels*, who, on account of their rebellious attitude, were expelled from the presence of God. Consequently, they constituted themselves into a kingdom of darkness always in direct opposition to the divine rule of God.

Thirdly, spiritual warfare is as old as the creation itself. It is an attempt on the part of Satan to struggle with God to lay claim to what does not belong to him. It is a concerted effort on the part of Satan and his cohorts to prevent man from finding fulfilment in his Creator. This he does by engaging all the powers at his disposal ('his angels' – Rev. 12:7), otherwise known as the *powers* and *principalities*, to cause man to disobey God always. He offers suggestions to man to make him believe that God does not love him as the word of God claims.

Even when the truth which is sufficient to set man free is presented, Satan comes in to take the same away, therefore keeping man in total darkness. For the Scripture says, 'And it happened as [the Sower] sowed, that some seed fell by the wayside; and the birds of the air came and devoured it…. And these are the ones by the wayside where the word is sown. And when they hear, Satan comes immediately and takes away the word that was sown in their hearts' (Mark 4:4,15).

In a nutshell, the *powers* and *principalities* are constituted *spiritual entities* in direct opposition to the divine rulership of God by means of contending the right of God to claim direct ownership of humanity. This is *spiritual warfare*, a matter of an ongoing battle between the Kingdom of God and kingdom of darkness. The battlefield is the heart of human beings, moral agents with the ability and free will to either obey or disobey God.

2

The Ministry of Paul in Ephesus
as a Prelude to Ephesians 6

Introduction

Paul's ideas and writings did not develop in a vacuum, and therefore are not mere products of his imagination. His writings are products of his life experiences in the course of preaching the gospel. It is important to stress this in order for us to be able to understand Paul's idea of spiritual warfare in his epistle to the Ephesians. For us to have a proper understanding of Ephesians 6:10-12, we must have a background knowledge of the situation in Ephesus so as to be able to appreciate Paul's message of salvation and the reason for the warnings he gives. We will need to consider the records in the book of the Acts because they prove helpful for 'providing a complementary source of information of a basically historical nature'.[1] In other words, 'such external information can help us to add credibility to whatever comes from the apostle himself'[2] in his epistle to the Ephesians.

The epistle to the Ephesians[3] was a product of Paul's contact with the city of Ephesus, and this contact resulted in the emergence of a new community, a congregation of predominantly Gentile believers in Christ. Paul states this clearly in Ephesians 2:11, 13, 19:

Therefore remember that you, once Gentiles in the flesh who are called Uncircumcision by what is called the Circumcision made in the flesh by hands, that at that time you were without Christ, being aliens from the commonwealth of Israel and strangers from the covenants of promise, having no hope and without God in the world. But now in Christ Jesus, you who once were far off have been made near by the blood of Christ. Now, therefore, you are no longer strangers and foreigners, but fellow citizens with the saints and members of the household of God.

In looking at the ministry of Paul among the Ephesians, a few probing questions are pertinent. What was the social setting of Ephesus at the time Paul ministered there? How did Paul get into their midst? What was the content of Paul's message? What influenced the Ephesians to accept the message that Paul preached to them? We shall also look at the effect of the message on the inhabitants of Ephesus, noting the power of the gospel and how his preaching brought about a new experience of salvation among the Ephesians. The answers to these questions should equip us to understand Paul's concept of spiritual warfare in Ephesians 6.

Our first assignment is to address *the social setting of the city of Ephesus at the time Paul ministered there*. A word of caution is appropriate here so that we do not confuse the issue we are trying to address with that of *the destination* or *provenance of the epistle*, which has attracted varied opinions among many scholars. Though this work does not attempt to engage in this debate, it will not be out of place to take a brief look into the question of whether the epistle was originally addressed to the Ephesians or it was meant to be a general circular letter. The purpose of this is to find out how our text in Ephesians 6 relates to Christians in Africa in the contemporary setting.

The question of the destination and purpose of the epistle is not easily resolved. This is because many ancient manuscripts do not include the words 'in Ephesus' (Eph. 1:1). This omission has made many scholars argue that the epistle was not originally sent to the Ephesians, but that rather it was a general circular letter, a Christian treatise composed for a general use; and written to the generality of the believers in Christian Churches in Asia Minor.

> As regards the implied readers of the original letter, we cannot be sure whether they were linked in the address with a particular church or churches in a specific city or cities. Not surprisingly, what is made clear from the outset however, is that they are to be seen as Christians.... A number of the images and descriptions used of the implied readers are corporate ones and make clear that they belong to a larger grouping of Christian believers, to the universal church. Somewhat more specifically, in terms of their ethnic background, these Christian readers who are part of the universal Church are

Gentiles. This identification is made explicit in the way they are addressed in 2:1 and 3:1, in the depiction of their past as religiously deprived in comparison with that of Israel (2:11-13), and in the reference to their past Gentile lifestyle in 4:17.[4]

The words 'at Ephesus' in Eph. 1. 1 might seem to put the destination of this letter beyond question, were it not for the fact that some of our earliest and weightiest authorities for the text omit these two words. It would be surprising, too, to have such an absence of personal references in a letter written by Paul to a church in whose midst he had spent the best part of three years. The most acceptable view, having regard to the general character of the letter, is that it was intended for all the churches of the province of Asia, some of which were personally known to Paul, while others were not (cf. Col. 2. 1). While the message of the letter was never intended to be limited to one local church only, we may quite justifiably call it 'The Epistle to the Ephesians', provided that we remember that it was sent also to other churches in the province of which Ephesus was the capital city.[5]

In reading other epistles such as 1 Corinthians, Galatians and Colossians, an enquirer may come up with suggestions of the issues being addressed based on the internal contents; in the case of Ephesians the task is not so easily identified. Even suggestions of Ephesians as a baptismal document[6] or an introduction to a collection of Paul's writings based on the reading of Acts[7] do not give a true reflection of the purpose for writing this epistle. In other words, the composition of Ephesians was not occasioned by any specific problems that can be identified from the contents of the book. Andrew Lincoln writes:

> It seems more appropriate, however, to respect the distinctiveness of this letter's lack of specificity by concentrating on the general implications of the letter and by being content with the correspondingly general contours of the setting that may be cautiously reconstructed.[8]

Adding more to the fact of the circular nature of this letter are the words of Ephesians 1:15: 'Therefore I also, after I heard of your faith in the Lord Jesus and your love for all the saints.' It is believed that Paul could not have written in such a way to people with whom he worked for almost three years and was well acquainted (Acts 20:31). This must have informed the view that the epistle to the Ephesians was actually written to the Laodiceans (Col. 4:16).

However, the argument in favour of the epistle to the Ephesians as *an encyclical document* is not easily resolved. If the epistle did start in its original form as a circular letter, there is no doubt that in the long run it came to be associated with the Ephesians. Going through the contents of the epistle, and juxtaposing that with what the book of the Acts reveals about the former life of the Ephesians, it could be well said that the contents of the epistle fit the situation of the people Paul ministered to in Ephesus. They were Gentiles, who were walking in darkness, manifesting a manner of life that was opposed to the righteousness of God (Eph. 2:11-12). But by grace, they were saved by faith on hearing the message of salvation (Eph. 2:8-9). In order for them not to go back to their old life of idolatry there is the need for them to be on their guard by fighting the battle of faith on a regular basis (Eph. 6:10-18).

The social setting of Ephesus
Having looked briefly at the destination and purpose of the epistle to the Ephesians, it is also necessary to consider the social setting of the city of Ephesus. Ephesus was in a strategic position as the commercial centre of Asia Minor. Markus Barth appropriately described the town as 'a city that was once outstanding among the harbours and trade centres of Asia Minor'.[9] Bruce gives a vivid description of the strategic location of the city:

Ephesus was [at the time of Paul's ministry] the greatest city of Asia Minor north of the Taurus range, although its harbour required constant dredging because of the alluvium carried down by the Caysterm at the mouth of which it stood. Standing on the main route from Rome to the east, it enjoyed political importance in addition to its geographical advantages: it was the seat of administration of the province of---, and at the same time a free Greek city, with its own senate and civic assembly; it was an assize town, and prided itself especially on its title 'Temple Warden of Artemis'.[10]

The magnificent temple of Diana located there was one of the seven wonders of the ancient world, a feature of which the inhabitants of the city were very proud (Acts 19:35). Closely related to this temple was the practice of magic and operation of the forces of darkness (Acts 19:19). Although the practice of magic was a common phenomenon in the entire Hellenistic world in the first century of the Christian faith, the city of Ephesus seemed to have exhibited an unparalleled reputation in this direction. 'Of all ancient Graeco-Roman cities, Ephesus, the third largest in the Empire, was by far the most hospitable to magicians, sorcerers, and charlatans of all sorts.'[11]

The book of Acts indicates that significant numbers of the dwellers of Ephesus were involved in the practice of magic and allied trades. It was from among this populace that Paul was able to make converts to the Lord, those who in turn demonstrated their total allegiance to the Lord Jesus Christ by burning their magical books. As noted by Arnold, the practice of magic in Ephesus existed side by side with the Christian faith in the early era of Christianity. This is evident in the fact that Christian prophecy was always directed against the magicians.[12] In other words, there were divinely motivated prophetic messages to dissuade new converts from lapsing into the practice of magic, a prevalent phenomenon in the city of Ephesus at that time.

In the light of its famous proverbial 'Ephesian Letters', which contained many written magical spells that were referenced in many Graeco-Roman secular writings,[13] Ephesus was indisputably known as a strategic magical centre. It is noteworthy that the contents of these Ephesian Letters are similar to the practice of magical power among Africans today.[14] These letters that were either used as 'written amulets' or 'spoken charms' were credited with powers that could ward off demonic spirits.[15]

The practice of magic, as rooted in the presence of the temple of the great goddess Diana, was a source of prosperity for the inhabitants of the city. This is evident from Acts 19:24-25: 'For a certain man named Demetrius, a silversmith, who made silver shrines of Diana, brought no small profit to the craftsmen. He called them together with the workers of similar occupation, and said,

"Men, you know that we have our prosperity by this trade." '

Thus, in terms of commercial, political and religious activities, Ephesus was a prosperous city. Just as its strategic location as the chief port city of Asia Minor accounted for its commercial prosperity, so also was it responsible for the importation of foreign religious practices of the surrounding nations to the town. Arnold observes:

> With Ephesus as the chief port city of Asia Minor there was frequent commercial contact between Ephesus and Alexandria. This had resulted in the dissemination of significant Egyptian religious influence in Ephesus which undoubtedly included the sharing of effective magical charms and recipes.[16]

It is obvious from the strategic location of the city of Ephesus that in the time of Paul it was a town greatly reputed. Thus according to Wesley Carr, 'At the time of Paul's visit Ephesus was again a key city, which, after its restoration from the preceding decades of trouble, was again exerting her civic autonomy.'[17] However, due to the gradual silting of the mouth of Kaystros River, a major linkage with this city, it lost all its importance in due course.[18]

From the Bible, there is not much we can know about Ephesus beyond the information given in the book of Acts.[19] One other source is 1 Timothy, written by Paul to Timothy, who was exercising his episcopal ministry at Ephesus (1 Tim. 1:3). Take, for instance, the injunction of Paul in 1 Timothy 6:6-10:

> But godliness with contentment is great gain. For we brought nothing into this world, and it is certain we can carry nothing out. And having food and clothing, with these we shall be content. But those who desire to be rich fall into temptation and a snare, and into many foolish and harmful lusts which drown men in destruction and perdition. For the love of money is a root of all kinds of evil, for which some have strayed from the faith in their greediness, and pierced themselves through with many sorrows.

We may be tempted to ask about the relevance of the above passage to the social setting of Ephesus. The answer is within our reach when juxtaposed with Acts 19:23-27. The congregation being pastored by Timothy included those who had given up their idolatrous way to walk in 'the Way'.[20] Could it be that those who had forsaken their old way of life were beginning to think about going back to what they have left behind? This is postulated since accumulation of wealth through magic might have proved an easier option for them (Acts 19:27), rather than God-given wealth (Deut. 8:18; cf. Prov. 10:22).

The fact that 'the love of money is a root of all evil' (1 Tim. 6:10) can be related to the mob action of the Ephesians as they seek to kill Paul and other converts (Acts 19:27-41), simply because their ill-gotten wealth by magic was under serious threat. In other words, the Ephesians could go to any length to acquire wealth, even if it meant taking the lives of other people. Their love of money may be quite evident in the fact that 'some have strayed from the faith in their greediness, and pierced themselves through with many sorrows' (1 Tim. 6:10).

Such an act may not be unconnected with the powers of darkness evident in the worship of the goddess Diana. This goddess could be conjured magically by the magicians to their own personal advantage, to bring some misfortune upon their victims, without thought about the accompanying disaster. Such is the essence of magic. In this direction, Arnold has noted the fundamental principle guiding the practice of magic in the Hellenistic world:

> The overriding characteristic of the practice of magic throughout the Hellenistic world was the cognisance of a spirit world exercising influence over virtually every aspect of life. The goal of the magician was to discern the helpful spirits from the harmful ones and learn the distinct operations and the relative strengths and authority of the spirits. Through this knowledge, means could be constructed (with spoken or written formulas, amulets, etc.) for the manipulation of the spirits in the interest of the individual person. With the proper formula, a spirit-induced sickness could be cured,…great harm could be brought to another person through the utterance of a curse.[21]

The city of Ephesus was highly susceptible to the operations of the power of darkness as evidenced in the practice of magic. This was so much so that a Christian needed to be in constant defence of the faith to be able to run the race set before him successfully. 'Fight the good fight of faith [in order to] lay hold on eternal life' (1 Tim. 6:12).

A brief look at the book of Revelation may also be helpful in our quest to establish the social setting of Ephesus. The church there is commended as labouring in the midst of those 'who are evil' and cannot bear the evil of those involved in the evil acts (Rev. 2:2). Are these evil ones to be equated with the magicians trading as silversmiths at the temple of the goddess Diana?

Paul's ministry in Ephesus

The next point to consider is the issue of how Paul penetrated the city of Ephesus with the gospel message. Paul's ministry there can be seen in three stages as recorded in the book of Acts. In each case, Paul's presence made a significant impact on the life of the inhabitants of the city.

The first visit of Paul to Ephesus

Paul's first contact with the city of Ephesus was at the end of his second missionary journey in the Autumn of A.D. 52, when he ministered briefly in the synagogue before he left for Jerusalem (Acts 18:18-21).[22] At this stage, he left behind Priscilla and Aquila, who were co-tentmakers (Acts 18:1-3).

Paul's ministry on his first visit to Ephesus was casual and successful, and it turned out to be a preparatory one. He visited the Jewish synagogue and reasoned with the Jews so well that 'they asked him to stay a longer time with them' (Acts 18:20). Paul did not yield to their request because he wanted to keep the 'coming feast in Jerusalem' (Acts 18:21). Yet he did say that he would return to Ephesus if God permitted him (Acts 18:21). Without any doubt, Paul's brief visit had made such a great impression on them that they would be ready to accommodate him should he visit them again.

The second visit of Paul to Ephesus

The second visit of Paul to Ephesus is recorded in Acts 19:1–20:1; this was during his third missionary journey. This time he ministered in the city for a period of two and half years, before departing in the Spring of A.D. 56. During this visit, he met a few believers, twelve in number, who were not completely strange to the things of 'the Way'. These 'disciples' had already experienced the baptism of John, which was 'a baptism of repentance' seeking its fulfilment by faith in Christ. The first assignment of Paul was to teach and baptise these disciples in the name of Christ. After baptising them, he also laid hands upon them for the gift of the Holy Spirit, which was immediately manifested as they spoke in tongues and prophesied (Acts 19:1-7).

Paul then engaged in a pattern of evangelism that would make the power of the gospel real to those in the city of Ephesus and beyond (Acts 19:10). This involved confronting the powers of darkness by taking the battle to the gate of the celebrated goddess Diana. Paul was so much involved in the preaching of the good news that he could not attend to every manner of sickness brought to him. However, people found release through 'unusual miracles by the hands of Paul, so that even handkerchiefs or aprons were brought from his body to the sick, and the diseases left them and the evil spirits went out of them' (Acts 19:11-12).

There are a few points to note here. First, it would seem as if the city of Ephesus was under heavy operation of the demonic forces. This point is further strengthened by the fact of the presence of some Jewish exorcists in the city. An exorcist is involved in the task of exorcising demonic spirits. This is a matter of command, the sole ingredient for making magic functional. The deities are petitioned by means of command to release power to ward off demonic spirits. This, of course, is not the power given by the Holy Spirit.

We should not be surprised by this practice. It was a regular practice not only among the Gentiles, but also among the Jews, as evident in Jesus' days. An exorcist, under the influence of a higher demonic power, would exorcise lesser demonic powers from the demonised person in a magically devised way (Acts 19:13). This was why the Pharisees were accusing Jesus Christ of casting out demons by Beelzebub, the ruler of the demons (Matt. 12:24).

The work of Clinton Arnold is very significant for understanding the various magical practices in existence among both the Hellenists and the Jews.[23] According to him:

Numerous strands of evidence point to the fact that the Judaism of the Hellenistic period had been heavily permeated by contemporary magical beliefs. It is often difficult to decide what is distinctively Jewish magic as opposed to syncretistic pagan magic which invokes Sabaoth or uses other Jewish motifs.[24]

One commonly cited extra-canonical writing which reflected the Jewish magical practices is the *Testament of Solomon*, which linked Solomon with the practice of magic, with ability to manipulate demonic spirits.[25] Magic was practised among the Jews, even though such actions were condemned by God (Deut. 18:9-12).

For magic to work, it depends on two major factors. First is the recitation of names of certain divinities by way of incantation to force their co-operation. Secondly, the gods are forcefully commanded to grant the request of the petitioners. Noting the usefulness of the magical papyri in this connection, Howard Kee has mentioned a few such names which include not only the divinities of the Graeco-Roman world, but those that are central to the Christian faith such as 'Logos, Jesus Christ, Holy Spirit, and Son of the Father'.[26] There is therefore no doubt that in the practice of magic among the Jews, the use of biblical and Christian terminologies, such as above, was very common. It might be possible that such a practice was in operation during the earthly ministry of Christ. Note His words:

> Not everyone who says to Me, Lord, Lord shall enter the kingdom of heaven, but he who does the will of My Father in heaven. Many will say to Me in that day, Lord, Lord, have we not prophesied in Your name, cast out demons in Your name, and done many wonders in Your name? And then I will declare to them, I never knew you; depart from Me, you who practice lawlessness (Matt. 7:21-23).

The fact that people used the name of Christ to cast out demons and to perform miracles would not be the measuring standard for knowing those who belong to Him. For miracles to be Christ-centred, those performing them have to confess Christ first, and then use the power that is in His name (Mark 16:17). But the words of Matthew 7 indicate that demonic agents performing miracles can still use the name of Jesus deceitfully.

Secondly, Paul had amazing success in the task of preaching the gospel in Ephesus. He presented the 'Power' of God in such a manner that the magicians around knew that they could not match the power working in him. This consequently led to the acknowledgement of 'the Jesus whom Paul preaches' (Acts 19:13). Exorcists knew that there were others, whose power cannot be compared to the power of the *real Jesus* whom Paul preaches. Take the account in Acts 13:

> Now when they had gone through the island to Paphos, they found a certain sorcerer, a false prophet, a Jew whose name was Bar-Jesus, who was with the proconsul, Sergius Paulus, an intelligent man. This man called for Barnabas and Saul and sought to hear the word of God. But Elymas the sorcerer (for so his name is translated) withstood them, seeking to turn the proconsul away from the faith. Then Saul, who also is called Paul, filled with the Holy Spirit, looked intently at him and said, 'O full of all deceit and all fraud, you son of the devil, you enemy of all righteousness, will you not cease perverting the straight ways of the Lord? And now, indeed, the hand of the Lord is upon you, and you shall be blind, not seeing the sun for a time.' And immediately a dark mist fell on him, and he went around seeking someone to lead him by the hand (Acts 13:6-11).

The magicians were making a great mistake. There is no way they could commercialise the name of Jesus for their selfish ends or personal aggrandisement. The name of Jesus is not magic. To know His power, one must be in relationship with Him. Paul was in relationship with Him, that is why he experienced the power that is in this name. Only those who have been declared righteous by the merit of the blood of Christ can use the power in the name to bring demonic forces to their knees.[27]

Thirdly, the ministry of Paul in Ephesus brought about great depopulation of the kingdom of darkness. Many converts were made from the magicians of the city, who gave up their magic to follow 'the Way': 'And many who had believed came confessing and telling their deeds. Also many of those who had practised magic brought their books together and burned them in the sight of all. And they counted up the value of them, and it totalled fifty thousand pieces of silver' (Acts 19:18-19). This is a great confirmation of the truth of the Scripture that 'the people who know their God shall be strong, and carry out great exploits' (Dan. 11:32b).

Regarding the life of the converts in Ephesus, there are three points to be noted. First, the new converts confessed their evil deeds. In other words, there was real acknowledgement of the fact that prior to their new faith in Christ, they were collaborators with Satan. While on the one hand they confessed their wicked acts of the past, on the other hand they confessed the Lordship of Christ over their lives.

Secondly, they brought forward all their demonic tools. This shows that there can be no secret disciples of the Lord Jesus Christ. They were not ashamed of identifying with Christ. They must have come to realise that previously they were weapons fashioned against the kingdom of God. The best way to disassociate themselves from the forces of darkness was by bringing forward their magical books to be burnt publicly.

Thirdly, there is the opposition of the kingdom of darkness to the spread of the gospel. Satan's sole aim in placing people under the bondage of demonic powers is to prey upon them regularly. Therefore any attempt made to liberate humans from his kingdom will be met with stiff opposition. Satan knew that he had lost total control over the lives of those he had previously kept under the bondage of magic and false religion in Ephesus. Was he going to leave it at that? Satan's intention was to strike back. He has a method, which is to incite people and cause them to rebel against anything that is godly and present his own diabolical agenda.

> And about that time there arose a great commotion about the Way. For a certain man named Demetrius, a silversmith, who made silver shrines of Diana, brought no small profit to the craftsmen. He called them together with the workers of similar occupation, and said, 'Men, you know that we have our prosperity by this trade. Moreover you see and hear that not only at Ephesus, but throughout almost all Asia, this Paul has persuaded and turned away many people, saying that they are not gods which are made with hands. So not only is this trade of ours in danger of falling into disrepute, but also the temple of the great goddess Diana may be despised and her magnificence

destroyed, whom all Asia and the world worship. And when they heard this, they were full of wrath and cried out, saying, 'Great is the Diana of the Ephesians' (Acts 19:23-28).

The magicians of Ephesus were bent on taking hold of the inhabitants of the city, to prevent them from knowing the truth so that they might not be saved. However, it was too late for them, for God had already added to His church those who were being saved. Through the preaching of Paul 'the word of the Lord [had grown] mightily and prevailed' (Acts 19:20), leading to the salvation of many souls. The church of God had come to stay in Ephesus; and the gates of hell could not prevail against it.

The third visit of Paul to Ephesus
Paul's third contact with Ephesus was his farewell meeting in Miletus with the elders of the Ephesian church when he was en-route to Jerusalem from Corinth (Acts 20:17-38). This encounter afforded Paul the opportunity to give a general overview of his three-year ministry in the city. From the account in Acts 20:17-38 we can learn a few more things about the church in Ephesus.

First, there was opposition to the ministry of Paul in the city of Ephesus, simply because he had exposed the wiles of the devil (Acts 20:19). The forces of darkness had not yet rested their case. Their intention was still to cause believers to backslide in order to make the gospel message of no effect (Acts 20:29).

Secondly, Paul knew that some of the elders were pretenders who had no genuine conversion experience. These were mere emissaries from the kingdom of darkness to lead believers back to their former sinful life. 'Also from among yourselves men will rise up, speaking perverse things, to draw away the disciples after themselves' (Acts 20:30). This prophecy seems to have been fulfilled before the sending of the letter in Revelation 2 to the church in Ephesus:

> To the angel of the church of Ephesus write, these things says He who holds the seven stars in His right hand, who walks in the midst of the seven golden lampstands: I know you works, your labour, your patience, and that you cannot bear those who are evil. And you

have tested those who say they are apostles and are not, and have found them liars (Rev. 2:1-2).

The presence of such false apostles can be related to Paul's admonition to the elders of the church to 'take heed to yourselves and to all the flock, among which the Holy Spirit has made you overseers, to shepherd the church of God which He purchased with His own blood' (Acts 20:28). In other words, the church in Ephesus must be guarded jealously so that the forces of darkness through their human agents would not be able to cause any spiritual derailment. Therefore, the leaders of the church must be firmly established in the faith.

Thirdly, the Christian faith had registered its permanent presence in Ephesus. Despite intense opposition God was establishing the faith of the Ephesian Christians. This was the purpose for which elders were appointed — 'to shepherd the church of God which He purchased with His own blood' (Acts 20:28b).

Conclusion

In concluding this chapter, it is necessary to reiterate the point that Paul's writings are a genuine product of his real life experiences. When he writes in his epistle to the Ephesians that 'we do not wrestle against flesh and blood, but against principalities, against powers, against the rulers of the darkness of this age, against spiritual hosts of wickedness in heavenly places' (Eph. 6:12), he is recalling his face-to-face encounter with the powers and principalities dressed in the garb of the magicians of the city of Ephesus and their followers.

Paul has an urgent message for the church at Ephesus. Though they have been rescued from the powers of darkness, the battle is not yet over. Hence, believers are to be on their guard, as demonstrated in the words of a hymn:

Christian seek not yet repose,
Hear thy guardian angels say,
Thou art in the midst of foes,
Watch and pray.[28]

3

Possible Sources for the Development and Use of Paul's Language of the Powers and Principalities

Introduction

Paul's life and ministry shaped a significant part of the New Testament. A careful survey demonstrates that the language of the powers and principalities is a dominant feature in his writings.[1] Caird believes that a 'very rapid survey of a dozen or more passages from the epistles [of Paul shows that] the concept of world powers reaches into every department of Paul's theology, and that it cannot be dismissed as a survival of primitive superstition.'[2] The purpose of this chapter therefore is to explore possible sources for the development and use of the distinctive language of the *powers* and *principalities* in Paul's thought. Should we take it for granted that Paul merely took over the Jewish tradition about the fallen angels (as treated in chapter one) as the antecedent to his language of the powers and principalities? But since Paul's writings were mostly directed to congregations in which the Gentiles constituted the majority, can we be sure that these Gentiles would have easily comprehended the foreign Jewish idea being presented to them? Or were there vestiges of this Jewish idea in the Graeco-Roman world of Paul's time which would have made the language intelligible to his audience?

Furthermore, should we agree with Schlier that, 'When they [powers and principalities] are mentioned by Jesus himself, or the apostles and the early Church, their hearers, whether Jewish or Gentile, knew what was meant?'[3] This is not an easy issue to resolve. Nevertheless, by looking at Paul's own Jewish background and the religious environment of the Graeco-Roman world of his time we may be able to discover what informed his use of the language of the powers and principalities in the context of the Christian faith.

There are various suggestions about the sources for the development of Paul's distinctive language of the powers and principalities. The work of Wesley Carr proves helpful in this direction. According to Carr, there are three possible suggestions.[4] First, there is the suggestion that Paul could have derived this concept from a recognisable Jewish source, which he later modified for his own use. Secondly, there is the suggestion that Christian sources contained such material in the time of Paul and that he merely had recourse to it. So in the view of Carr, 'Paul entered upon a Christian tradition that was already advanced in its process of formulation.'[5] Thirdly, since the exercise of Paul's ministry in the first century was mainly in Asia Minor, it has been suggested that Paul's contact with the prevailing cultures of his different audiences must have informed his use of the language of the powers and principalities.

However, after a careful examination of these suggested sources, Carr seems to leave his readers in the state of indecision. It looks as if he wants his readers carefully to weigh all the options at their disposal based on his presentation, and make up their minds as to which option is most tenable. He writes:

> The background to Paul's language and thought, therefore, is not simply to be sought in Palestine or in Judaism, for his life was lived in the main apart from the developing political and social unrest of that province.... Nor, on the other hand, is the source of his language to be sought in the realms of mysteries and astrology. These were at the time of his mission at a low ebb and use of any technical language derived from them, even if it was known to Paul, would have conveyed little to his readers.[6]

It is my task, therefore, in this section to demonstrate that both Jewish and Hellenistic religious environments of Paul's day coupled with his own personal experience on the mission field were the significant backgrounds for the development of his distinctive language of the powers and principalities. In other words, neither of the two religious backgrounds nor the existing Christian tradition was sufficient to account for the development of Paul's distinctive language of the powers and principalities.

Thus, an eclectic approach is preferred, as will be demonstrated in what follows.

The Jewish religious background

Although Paul was a Hellenistic Jew, he was not a stranger to the Jewish tradition that strongly believed in the concept of the national guardian angels. Israel was a nation brought into a covenant relationship with God, a people preferred by God above all other nations on the earth. The term of this covenant was that they must always remain faithful to Him without serving any other gods. 'And God spoke all these words, saying, I am the LORD your God, who brought you out of the land of Egypt, out of the house of bondage. You shall have no other gods before Me' (Exod. 20:1-2). It is quite obvious in the Old Testament that the people of Israel repeatedly broke this term of their covenant agreement with God by worshipping the gods of their surrounding nations.

In the words of Deuteronomy, God warned them:

> And take heed, lest you lift your eyes to heaven, and when you see the sun, the moon, and the stars, all the host of heaven, you feel driven to worship them and serve them, which the LORD your God has given to all the peoples under the whole heaven as a heritage (Deut. 4:19).

The sun, moon and stars were created by God (Gen. 1:16), and were given to mankind to enjoy, and not to be worshipped. Israel's later calamities were predicated upon this single cause, forsaking God and serving the gods of other surrounding nations. This syncretism necessitated the prophetic ministries of the prophets of both the pre-exilic and exilic periods, calling the Israelites to return to the only true God by forsaking the powerless gods who could not save them.

In later Jewish writings, it would seem as if the concept of individual national angels had developed into astral powers trying to battle for supremacy. Thus we read from the book of Daniel:

> Then he said to me, 'Do not fear, Daniel, for from the first day that you set your heart to understand, and to humble yourself before your God, your words were heard; and I come because of your words. But the prince of the kingdom of Persia withstood me twenty-one days;

and behold, Michael, one of the chief princes, came to help me, for I had been left alone there with the kings of Persia....' Then he said, 'Do you know why I have come to you? And now I must return to fight with the prince of Persia; and when I have gone forth, indeed the prince of Greece will come' (Dan. 10:13, 20).

These words indicate that there was an ensuing battle between the guardian angels of two nations. There was also the appearance of the third angel, the archangel Michael, sent by God to defend His people. In the context of national guardian angels, the appearance of the two angels in the above text was synonymous with the nations they represented. The idea was not strange either in the inter-testamental period, as attested to in the extra canonical literature, where Israel is subject to God alone, but other nations to angels.

> For all the angels of the presence and all the angels of sanctification have been created from the day of their creation, and before the angels of the presence and the angels of sanctification He hath sanctified Israel, that they should be with Him and with His holy angels...for there are many nations [and] many peoples, and all are His, and over all hath He placed spirits in authority to lead them astray from Him. But over Israel He did not appoint any angel or spirit, for He alone is their ruler, and He will preserve them and require them at the hand of His angels and His spirits, and at the hand of all His powers in order that He may preserve them and bless them, and that they may be His and He may be theirs from henceforth for ever (Jubilees 15:27,31-32).[7]

It is noteworthy that early Christianity was not at variance with late Judaism in respect of the view that unseen powers were in operation behind the cosmic events. This was to be understood in the fact of a firm belief in the presence of the angels of the nations as discussed earlier in the context of Daniel 10. Such a belief would explain the reason for emphasising the need to bring the *powers* and *principalities* into subjection to the Lordship of Christ. This is a dominant theme in Paul's writings and it occupies a central place in Pauline theology. Caird, writing to this end, says:

It was a common phenomenon in the ancient world for a deity to be the personification of the state over which he presided; and, under the successive domination of Babylon, Persia, Greece, and Rome, Israel was to have ample opportunity to discover that the pagan empires, whether they were symbolised by their earthly kings of by their heavenly guardians, constituted a power to be reckoned with.[8]

The point here is to demonstrate that it was God who created the whole of the universe and was in charge of whatever guardian spirits He appointed for the nations. This is to keep Israel from undue pride and to let them know that their election was a great privilege that must be responded to with a corresponding obedience.

The Hellenistic religious background

Our discussion here will take the form of a response to the view of Carr as noted earlier. There is the need for clarification of Carr's earlier submission in the way he relegated the Hellenistic religious system in the arena of Paul's ministry. In other words, it cannot be easily accepted that the concept of 'mysteries and astrology...at the time of his mission [were] at a low ebb and [the] use of any technical language derived from them, even if it was known to Paul, would have conveyed little to his readers'.[9] The language of Acts 14 is a clear indication that the concept of astral powers was very much rooted in the Hellenistic religious environment at the time of Paul's missionary journey. The inhabitants of Asia Minor were not only used to them, but also demonstrated that the astral powers were of great significance for knowing the mighty acts of the unseen powers. This is quite evident in Paul's encounter with the residents of Lystra:

> Now when the people saw what Paul had done, they raised their voices, saying in the Lycaonian language, 'The gods have come down to us in the likeness of men.' And Barnabas they called Zeus, and Paul Hermes, because he was the chief speaker. Then the priest of Zeus, whose temple was in front of their city, brought oxen and garlands to the gates, intending to sacrifice with the multitudes (Acts 14:11-12).

While we are not suggesting that the tradition operating in the

Hellenistic mystery religions was the bedrock of Paul's language of the powers and principalities, a point that was rightly noted by Carr, yet, for Paul to have used such language, it is our contention that his audience was quite familiar with the tradition existing in their religious environment.

In other words, it is misleading to claim that 'mysteries and astrology...at the time of his mission [were] at a low ebb and use of any technical language derived from them, even if it was known to Paul, would have conveyed little to his readers.'[10] Noting the prevalence of the concept of the astral powers and allied evil forces in the Graeco-Roman world at the time of Paul, Arnold writes:

> ...virulent spiritual forces were perceived by the first century inhabitants of western Asia Minor as troubling their daily existence. Artemis, amulets, charms and various other forms of apotropaic magic were appealed to and utilised for relief from diabolical tyranny.[11]

Paul lived his life in the Graeco-Roman environment where the concept of astral powers was a dominant factor in the religious life of the people. Paul, being a Jew, must have known as a matter of tradition that the worship of these astral powers constituted a great threat to the worship of the only supreme and true God of the Jews.

In this connection, it is important to consider the Septuagint, which offers a convenient link between Hebrew and Greek thought, by looking at some of the words it uses. Mention of the powers and principalities is found therein. According to Caird, 'it is here that we find the terms *powers* [*dunameis*], *authorities* [*exousiai*], *principalities* [*archai*] and *rulers* [*archontes*] applied for the first time to angelic beings.... Where the Hebrew speaks of God's hosts, the Greek sometimes speaks instead of his powers.'[12]

Knowing fully that Paul was a man of two worlds (Hebrew and Greek), we recognise that his concept of the powers and principalities is reminiscent of the understanding of the gods of the Greek pantheon operating at a lower level under the supreme authority of the only one true God, which is a major Jewish concept (Exod. 20:1-3). According to Macgregor:

Such astral beliefs had, of course, long ago found a place in religion, as one way of explaining the continued existence of the of the heathen alongside of the One God, Yahweh. Pagan wors but star-worship, the worship of the creature rather than the creato

The point is that, as a Jew, Paul knew that the pantheon of the surrounding nations could not be placed on the same pedestal as the Hebrew God. The pantheon might be worshipped and appealed to for powers, but such powers were no powers before the God of Israel. Therefore, there is no doubt that Paul's Greek environment had tremendous influence on him in the sense that he was able to distinguish between the authentic and inauthentic powers that could exercise control over humankind. Noting this great influence Macgregor again writes:

> When discussing Paul's references to 'principalities and powers' and the relation of his thought to contemporary astral religious beliefs we must certainly have this Old Testament background constantly in view. But we shall remember too that although the source of such ideas is undoubtedly to be found far back in Chaldaean astrological lore, by Paul's day Jewish thought had already been strongly infected by influences, philosophical and religious, which were Hellenistic rather than Semitic.[14]

In the Greek pantheon the seven planets are personified as rulers of this world and discerners of human fate. In the Hellenistic culture it was believed that peoples' lives were controlled by the astral powers, which were the elemental spirits of the universe. The devotees of these astral gods worshipped them as *rulers*. The future of a person was decided by the predictions based on the star at the time of birth. Astrology was central to the religious life of the Greeks. Closely connected to the astral powers is the notion of magic, a way for a stronger demonic power to force its own will on the less powerful one. In magic, humans learn the secrets hidden in the forces operating in the universe through mysterious communications in nature.

While there was no obvious reason to suggest that Paul was at any time under such bondage, it must be remarked that he was quite familiar with such a practice on the mission field as evident

ts. He knew the wickedness of these astral-
...ed the believers in Ephesus that 'we do
...and blood, but against principalities,
...e rulers of the darkness of this age, against
...ickedness in the heavenly places' (Eph. 6:12).
...ave called to remembrance his encounter with the
...ans of the city of Ephesus, the subsequent conversion of
...ome among them and the burning up of their magical
instruments.[15]

Indeed, Paul knew that in the magicians of the city of Ephesus
the powers of darkness were at work. These powers were constantly
motivating the priests and other devotees of the Temple of Diana
to bring people into the bondage of the dark powers.

Paul's use of the language of the powers and principalities

Having identified the sources of Paul's distinctive language of the
powers and the *principalities*, it is essential that we attempt a careful
examination of his use of the same. It is our contention that Paul
had a different intention when he used the terms *powers* and
principalities. His language of the powers and principalities is to
be understood in relation to the new life of a believer under the
surveillance of emissaries from the kingdom of darkness seeking
to cause spiritual derailment. More than often, the kingdom of
darkness operates through institutionalised bodies such as the state
or government co-operating together to perpetrate wicked acts.
For the purpose in view, we shall look presently at two selected
texts from Paul's writings – Romans 8 and 1 Corinthians 2.
(Ephesians 6:12 and Colossians 2:15 will receive attention in
chapters 5 and 8.) What we are seeking to do here is to demonstrate
that Paul's use of the language of the powers and principalities in
Romans 8 and 1 Corinthians 2 lends credence to his later use of
the same in Ephesians 6 and Colossians 2. In other words, the four
passages belong together in Paul's thought world.

Reference to the principalities and powers in Romans 8:37-39

In this text, Paul's main objective was to reassure the believers in
the church at Rome about the certainty of the victory already won

for them by Christ through His death and resurrection (Rom. 6:1-4). The way he chose to this was by reminding them that they remain inseparable from Christ, into whom they have been incorporated and who has thus made the power of God real to them. Here, Paul writes:

> Yet in all these things we are more than conquerors through Him who loved us. For I am persuaded that neither death nor life, nor angels nor principalities nor powers, nor things present nor things to come, nor height nor depth, nor any other created thing, shall be able to separate us from the love of God which is in Christ Jesus our Lord (Rom. 8:37-39).

A proper understanding of this passage is rooted in the first section of verse 35, 'Who shall separate us from the love of Christ?' In other words, the new life of the believer is a condition that has attracted the obvious attention from the kingdom of darkness, and there are forces of darkness seeking to separate the believer from the source of this new life. The intention of the dark kingdom is to take believers back to the old life of the sinful nature (Rom. 6:1; cf. Eph. 2:1-3).

The mention of *principalities* and *powers* in addition to other forces, especially *angels*, seeking to 'separate' believers 'from the love of Christ' or 'from the love of God which is in Christ Jesus' places the duo in the realm of unseen negative spiritual forces working against the plan of God to redeem mankind. Thus for Paul, the powers and principalities are in the realm of *concrete spiritual entities* regularly holding sway over mankind. The view of John Murray in relation to these entities is helpful:

> That preternatural beings are in view need not be questioned. The word 'angels' can be used of evil spirits, angels that kept not their first estate (cf. Matt. 25:41; 2 Peter 2:4; Jude 6).... 'Principalities' is used in the New Testament of both good (Col. 1:16; 2:10) and evil (Eph. 6:12; Col. 2:15). Hence 'principalities' could readily, according to Paul's usage, refer to the principalities of wickedness.[17]

In a similar way, with the use of powers in this text, Murray has observed that 'powers' as a term is frequently associated with 'angels' and 'principalities' and it is regarded as referring to preternatural beings.[18]

While we concur with Murray's view of the negative interpretations of 'principalities' in the above text, we however find it difficult to agree with his view that Paul had a good use of the same in his writings. Paul's use of 'principalities' in all the above references is from the negative point of view, especially when juxtaposed with Colossians 2:15 – they are brought into subjection to the reign of Christ. Since they are presently acting at cross-purposes to the will of God in the present age, judgement awaits them at the second coming of Christ.

Murray's view partly corroborates that of Carr who did not interpret the powers and principalities as forces of darkness, but instead saw them as good and acceptable in the services of God:

> The language of [*archai*],[*exousiai*]and [*dynameis*], when it does occur in Jewish writings, seems not to be found in the distinctively Pauline configuration of [*archai*] and [*exousiai*]. More significant, however, is the fact that the words are confined to the angels and archangels of Yahweh, and never are used of demonic forces.[19]

Carr's agenda is primarily to demonstrate the ministry of the angels in Jewish understanding from the positive point of view. Hence, whatever runs counter to his idea must either be rejected or reworked to fit into his structured agenda. While Carr may be correct to some extent in seeing the ministry of the angels from a positive point of view, since some of them were bringers of good news (Matt. 1:20-21; Luke 1:11-17, 26-33), yet it must be noted that Paul's use of the language of the powers and principalities does not permit such an exclusive interpretation.

A quick glance at the related passages containing Paul's language of the powers and principalities shows that the notion of earthly structures (by way of state, government or individual government functionary) does not help to understand this important Pauline concept in the context of his overall theology (cf. 1 Cor. 15:24-28; Gal. 4:3,9; Eph. 1:20-21; 3:10; 6:10-12; Col. 1:16; 2:10, 15).[20] In other words, the use of this language was not simply politically motivated. Rather, when Paul employed the language of the powers and principalities, he was combating the forces of the dark kingdom that had the nature of spiritual beings. Though not seen, they manifest themselves as beings of intellect and will, who can speak and be spoken to. Examples of this fact abound in the New Testament – demons speak in the synagogue (Mark 1:23), and when they are to be cast out (Mark 5:1-12).

These spiritual entities may not be seen, yet they do operate in concrete ways. Although intangible, their activities can be felt. (This will be discussed more in chapter 7, where we will present Christ as the only Power who can deliver from the clusters of demonic forces.) It should be noted meantime that for Paul the concept of the 'powers and principalities' is not a mere apocalyptic imagination.[21] Stewart observes the need to focus on the reality of the presence of the powers and principalities in the theology of the entire New Testament, but notes in particular that the theme is an integral part of Paul's overall theology. Paul, while on the mission field, knew the aggressiveness of these evil forces that were always seeking to thwart his God-given mission. He was not speaking of ordinary political, economic or social institutions as opposing him. Rather, for him, these institutions were effective channels for the kingdom of darkness to manifest its powers.

The principalities and powers in 1 Corinthians 2:7-8

Paul writes, 'But we speak the wisdom of God in a mystery, the hidden wisdom which God ordained before the ages for our glory, which none of the rulers of this age knew; for had they known, they would not have crucified the Lord of glory' (1 Cor. 2:7-8). The main issue in this text centres on 'the rulers of this age' who crucified Christ in ignorance. Herod and Pilate represented the civil authority. They were the rulers of the day and thus constituted the powers to be reckoned with. It amounts to mere foolishness to think that Herod and Pilate, who represented the state, were merely acting on their own volition without the forces of darkness operating through them. Paul knew that for them to act in that way, they had sold themselves over to 'the rulers of the darkness of this age'.

So for Paul, the state can be demonised through its leaders manifesting the wickedness of the dark kingdom in concrete acts such as the crucifixion of Christ. In this sense, Stewart writes:

> Herod and Pilate, the representatives of government, the duly
> constituted [*archontes*] of the day, were unwitting agents of powers
> greater than their own, greater even than the Roman State, namely
> the invisible, spiritual, demonic [*archontes tou aionos toutou*]: it was
> they...[who crucified Jesus Christ, the Lord of glory].[22]

Therefore, when Paul speaks of civil authority such as in
Romans 13:1, he does not merely think about men in civil authority,
administering the day to day affairs of the populace, but rather he
takes into consideration the angelic powers (forces of darkness)
operating in the background and ruling through these civil
authorities. As noted by O'Brien, when appraising the work of
Cullmann, 'Whenever [*exousiai*] occurs in the Pauline letters in
the plural or in the plurally used singular with [*pasa*] (except for
Tit. 3:1) it clearly signifies invisible angelic powers (1 Cor. 15:24;
Eph. 1:21; 3:10; 6:12; Col. 1:16; 2:10,15; cf. 1 Pet. 3:22).[23]

In the light of the above, there is therefore the need to understand
the mind of Paul before attempting to interpret him. This caution
is essential to guide against interpreting Paul within the confines
of human institution and structures, as some of the theologians of
the post World War II attempted to do.[24] Noting this wider structural
interpretation, O'Brien writes:

> As a post-war theory it assumed that when the apostle Paul spoke of
> the 'principalities and powers', as well as equivalent terms, he was
> alluding to structures of thought such as tradition, convention, law,
> authority and even religion, particularly as embodied in the state and
> its institutions, rather than to demonic intelligences.'[25]

For Paul, the language of the powers and principalities is not an
abstract one. While tradition, law, authority and religion are all
recognised human, political or religious institutions in Paul's
thought, yet if any of these constitutes a system that impinges on
God's sovereignty, this can only be explained in view of the fact
that forces of darkness are operating through such an institution.
Whenever this language is employed,

Paul has in view demonic intelligence of a much higher order... who possessed the poor disordered souls that meet us in the Gospel pages. These are cosmic spirit forces which possess and control not only individual human lives but the very course of the universe.[26]

In other words, Paul knew that these forces of darkness could operate through human, political and religious institutions to affect the course of humanity. The point being made is that these civil authorities have no inherent wickedness in them, save in the human agents acting as their functionaries. Civil institutions are wicked simply because the forces of darkness are operating through human beings who are designated agents.

Conclusion

At this juncture it is important to sum up our discussion in relation to the various backgrounds responsible for the emergence of Paul's distinctive language of the powers and principalities, and the use of the same among his listeners.

First, we noted that Paul was not a stranger to the concept of the powers and principalities in both Jewish and Gentile thought. In light of this, Paul was able to present his message knowing that his audiences would be able to decode his language of communication.

Secondly, we observed the view that credited these angelic beings with positive functions and therefore maintained that the *powers* and *principalities* are in good standing in the service of God. It is our belief that Paul did not hold such a view. There is no doubt that Paul has a positive view of angelic beings, but these are the angels in the service of God as ministering spirits. An example was during Paul's last journey to Rome when there was a shipwreck because the officials disobeyed Paul's advice to sail out from Fair Havens, near the city of Lasea:

> But after long abstinence from food, then Paul stood in the midst of them and said, 'Men, you should have listened to me, and not have sailed from Crete and incurred this disaster and loss. And now I urge you to take heart, for there will be no loss of life among you, but only of the ship. For there stood by me this night an angel of the God to

whom I belong and whom I serve, saying, "Do not be afraid, Paul;
you must be brought before Caesar; and indeed God has granted you
all those who sail with you." Therefore take heart, men, for I believe
God that it will be just as it was told me' (Acts 27:21-25).

Thirdly, we noted the view that tends to interpret Paul's
language of the powers and principalities from a mere political
and civil point of view, which seems very unlikely to be an adequate
representation of Paul's original intention. It is our contention,
based on the contextual settings of his message, that such an idea
would be foreign to the apostle .

We are convinced that Paul's Jewish background (with its
understanding of the concept of angelic powers as national guardian
spirits), his Hellenistic background (with the Greek idea of astral
powers as rulers under the authority of God), and his own
interaction with his mixed audiences on the mission field within
their cultural settings enabled him to fashion out his distinctive
language of the *powers* and *principalities*. Thus whenever he speaks
of the principalities and powers, he is to be understood as
confronting constituted authorities acting in defiance of the divine
rulership of the living God.

4

Paul's Understanding of Satanic Weapons of Spiritual Warfare

Introduction

The present chapter is central to this study. From chapters one to three we have attempted to lay a proper foundation that will enable us to appreciate Paul's strand of thought when it comes to the operation of the forces of darkness seeking to frustrate the believer's new life as he or she runs the Christian race. For Paul, the Christian life is not a dormant one. While something has happened by way of liberation from the captivity of Satan (salvation), yet the devil is not at rest, he seeks many other ways to bring the believer back into bondage (backsliding). This is the sense in which the Scripture speaks of Satan as the devil who walks about like a roaring lion, seeking whom he may devour (1 Pet. 5:8).

As we approach our discussion here, two points will be noted. First, what is Paul's view of warfare? In other words, does Paul have any concrete idea of spiritual warfare in his teachings or is such an idea a mere imposition of his interpreters? If he does, what necessitated this? Secondly, we shall also attempt to find out the identity of the opponents of Paul, and the weapons[1] at their disposal to wage the war.

As we examine the above points, our discussion will be undertaken in the context of a few selected texts from the letters of Paul, by way of substantiating what we believe to be his understanding of spiritual warfare and the weapons at the disposal of the enemy to fight the same.

Paul's view of spiritual warfare

Paul was a man highly sensitive to the needs of his converts. This point will be stressed at various stages in this chapter for the sake of emphasis, and should not be seen as a mere tautology. Paul knew the serious implications of what it means to change ownership, a transfer from one kingdom to another, a translation from the kingdom of darkness into the kingdom of light. Paul's admonition to the Ephesian Christians is a clear demonstration of this fact:

> Therefore remember that you, once Gentiles in the flesh who are called Uncircumcision by what is called Circumcision made in the flesh by hands, that at that time you were without Christ, being aliens from the commonwealth of Israel and strangers from the covenants of promise having no hope and without God in the world. But now in Christ Jesus you who once were far off have been made near by the blood of Christ (Eph. 2:11-13).

Elsewhere Paul writes, 'Therefore, if anyone is in Christ, he is a new creation; old things have passed way; behold, all things have become new' (2 Cor. 5:17). Paul was not an idealist, rather he was a man who allowed his experience to bear on his writings.

Paul confessed his ignorance while operating in the kingdom of darkness, thinking that he, as a Jew was defending the righteousness of the God of his fathers, 'concerning the law, a Pharisee; concerning zeal, persecuting the church' (Phil. 3:5b-6a). Paul had acted in ignorance simply by persecuting the church insofar as he had persecuted Christians whom he thought were preaching 'an accursed of God' (Deut. 21:23).

Later, Paul discovered why he could not understand that he was acting against the will of God when persecuting the early Christians. The reason is that 'the natural man does not received the things of the Spirit of God, for they are foolishness to him; nor can he know them, because they are spiritually discerned' (1 Cor. 2:14). The phrase 'the natural man' implies *man in his unregenerate form*, and this adequately describes Paul in his pre-conversion experience. He was an unregenerate man working in partnership with the forces of darkness. As an ardent Pharisee, he was co-operating with the established religious and political institutions of his time to unleash havoc on their perceived enemies – the Christians. This was quite evident in the role he played in the death of the first Christian martyr Stephen:

> Then they [the Jews] cried out with a loud voice, stopped their ears, and ran at him [Stephen] with one accord; and they cast him out of the city and stoned him. And the witnesses laid down their clothes at the feet of a young man named Saul. As for Saul, he made havoc of the church, entering every house, and dragging off men and women, committing them to prison (Acts 7:57-58; 8:3).

It is obvious from the above texts that Paul was a key figure who played a prominent role in the persecution of the believers in the teething period of the Christian faith. In other words, demonic forces found a ready tool in the person of Paul of Tarsus (who was previously known as Saul).[2]

> Then Saul, still breathing threats and murder against the disciples of the Lord went to the high priest and asked letters from him to the synagogues of Damascus, so that if he found any who were of the Way, whether men or women, he might bring them bound to Jerusalem (Acts 9:1).

While Paul was in full co-operation with the demonic forces behind the religious institutions of his time, there was no cause for him to be persecuted, since a kingdom does not seek to be divided against itself in the way it operates. But shortly after he had left those religious institutions in the event of his conversion experience, he started encountering opposition from the groups that he had earlier identified with. 'But Saul increased all the more in strength, and confounded the Jews who dwelt in Damascus, proving that this Jesus is the Christ. Now after many days were past, the Jews plot to kill him' (Acts 9:22-23).

The point of emphasis here is that Paul knew that the Christian life involves spiritual warfare. This spiritual warfare has three significant implications. We will examine each of these implications in what follows, so as to be sensitive enough to the goings on in the kingdom of darkness for us to be able to put up an aggressive defence of the faith.

First, the kingdom of darkness battles with believers and seeks to bring them back to unbelief, as is demonstrated in the case of Demas, once an associate of Paul (Col. 4:14). The last Pauline comment on Demas is a disheartening one: 'for Demas has forsaken me, having loved this present world' (2 Tim. 4:10). Demas had become a backslider through the cunning wiles the devil always employs, that is, 'the lust of the flesh, the lust of the eyes, and the pride of life' (1 John 2:16). Herein lies the full implication of the seeds that fell by the wayside, and into the midst of the thorns, in the parable of the sower:

> And these are the ones by the wayside where the word is sown. And when they hear, Satan comes immediately and takes away the word that was sown in their hearts. Now these are the ones sown among the thorns; they are the ones who hear the word, and the cares of this world, the deceitfulness of riches, and the desires for other things entering in choke the word, and it becomes unfruitful (Mark 4:15, 18-19).

Secondly, the kingdom of darkness is relentlessly seeking to terminate abruptly the life of believers if they are not on guard. In Revelation 12:17, 'the dragon was enraged with the woman, and he went to make war with the rest or her offspring, who keep the commandments of God and have the testimony of Jesus Christ.'

An example may be found in Samson. He was chosen for a great purpose, but because he was not watchful enough his days were cut short (Judg. 16:28-30). That is not to say that such believers will not make it to heaven. Certainly they will, for the Epistle to the Hebrews attests to the name of Samson in the hall of faith (Heb. 11:32). Yet such believers may not finish their God-given assignment before their death, in the way that apostle Paul testified to have finished his race.

It is worth noting that though on one occasion Paul had expressed his wish to depart from this earth to go and be with Christ, he knew that he had not finished his God-given assignment and that the infant church would require more of his evangelistic and pastoral supports:

> For to me, to live is Christ, and to die is gain. But if I live on in the flesh, this will mean fruit from my labour; yet what I shall choose I cannot tell. For I am hard pressed between the two, having a desire to depart and be with Christ, which is far better. Nevertheless to remain in the flesh is more needful for you (Phi. 1:21-24),

In other words, Paul wanted to remain on the earth until the appointed time for his final departure when he would have completed all that God had given him to do (2 Tim. 4:7). For Paul, even though the enemy might be raging and devising many means to stop him from running the race to the expected end (2 Cor. 12:23-27), he was not going to quit the stage until he had fully completed his task.

Thirdly, the kingdom of darkness may wage many wars seeking either to pull back or terminate the lives of the believers, yet if such believers steadfastly resist the forces from the kingdom of darkness, the devil will flee. 'Therefore submit to God. Resist the devil and he will flee from you' (James 4:7). Paul brings this out clearly as he writes, 'Put on the whole armour of God, that you may be able to stand against the wiles of the devil. Therefore take up the whole armour of God, that you may be able to withstand in the evil day, and having done all, to stand' (Eph. 6:11, 13). Paul knew that the Christian life is not a bed of roses. While the believer's justification rooted in Christ's death is 'once for all' (Rom. 6:11), yet growth in the new life is on a continuous basis, 'until we all come to the unity of the faith and the knowledge of the Son of God, to a perfect man, to the measure of the stature of the fullness of Christ' (Eph. 4:13).

Therefore, in response to our earlier question as to whether or not Paul has any concrete idea of spiritual warfare, our answer is in the affirmative. Paul knows that the Christian life is total warfare. The believer must defend on a regular basis his new life. Thus, 'While enjoying God's grace in this condition of freedom, he must be alive to God in Christ and continue to fight the Christian battle daily so as to present himself to God as a living sacrifice.'[3] Paul knows that spiritual warfare is not a matter of employing physical weapons since the battle is not in the physical arena. With this in view, he writes to the Ephesians, 'For we do not wrestle against flesh and blood, but against principalities, against powers, against the rulers of the darkness of this age, against spiritual hosts of wickedness in the heavenly places' (Eph. 6:12).[4]

Immediately after his conversion, Paul must have understood that he was in for a serious lifelong battle with the forces of darkness. He must have known that the Christian life is a race that must be run without allowing the distractions of the enemies to cause him any derailment. He knew that there was a prize of eternal crown of righteousness awaiting him if only he fought rightly, finished his race successfully and was able to keep the faith intact as a victorious Christian. The Scripture leaves us in no doubt of this fact. Towards the end of his ministry, having achieved this he writes:

> For I am already being poured out as a drink offering, and the time of my departure is at hand. I have fought the good fight, I have finished the race, I have kept the faith. Finally, there is laid up for me the crown of righteousness (2 Tim. 4:6-8).

Paul, at different points in his missionary journeys, met with different oppositions in the form of religious and civil institutions (Acts 16:16-24), which aimed at thwarting the plan of God for his life, by simply trying to prevent him from fulfilling what God had appointed him for.

Paul had had a very fruitful ministry in Thessalonica to the disappointment of the devil. The book of Acts has a vivid account of Paul's ministry there:

> Now when they had passed through Amphipolis and Apollonia, they came to Thessalonica, where there was a synagogue of the Jews. Then Paul, as his custom was, went in to them, and for three Sabbaths reasoned with them from the Scriptures, explaining and demonstrating that the Christ had to suffer and rise again from the dead, and saying, 'This Jesus whom I preach to you is the Christ.' And some of them were persuaded; and a great multitude of the devout Greek, and not a few of the leading women, joined Paul and Silas (Acts 17:1-4).

Paul's ministration at Thessalonica brought great defeat to the kingdom of darkness so much so that many were added to the body of Christ. This had caused a great uproar in the kingdom of darkness. Satan was greatly disturbed. He must respond by trying to bring up false accusation against Paul and his companions just to discredit the gospel they had preached in the city:

> The Jews who were not persuaded, becoming envious, took some of the evil men from the market place, and gathering a mob, set all

the city in an uproar and attacked the house of Jason, and sought to bring them out to the people. But when they did not find them, they dragged Jason and some brethren to the rulers of the city, crying out, 'These who have turned the world upside down have come here too' (Acts 17:5-6).

According to Paul's mission strategy, he always went back to the cities where he had preached the gospel in order to encourage his converts by way of effective follow-up (Acts 18:23). After the initial mission many attempts were made by Paul to visit again the believers in Thessalonica, but he was greatly resisted by Satan, who did not want a consolidation of the good work the Lord had begun among the Thessalonians. This is evident in Paul's letter to the church there:

> But we, brethren, having been taken away from you for a short time in presence, not in heart, endeavoured more eagerly to see your face with great desire. Therefore we wanted to come to you – even I, Paul, time and again – but Satan hindered us (1 Thess. 2:17-18).

Paul knew that it was not only human beings who were preventing him from coming to the believers in Thessalonica, but the forces of darkness operating through them. The resistance to Paul was by satanic agents. Indeed, this was a battle, and Paul knew what it meant to wrestle with such forces of darkness. Paul knew that the human agents trying to prevent him from doing what God had purposed for him were emissaries from the kingdom of darkness. As noted by O'Brien, 'the demons, spirits, angels, principalities and powers are regarded as subordinate to Satan or the devil. They are his innumerable powers seen as organised into a single empire. They are manifestations of the devil's power.'[5] Thus, while to an ordinary eye, the 'Jews', mere men, were responsible for stirring up the uproar in Thessalonica and even putting up the resistance against Paul, yet the fact remains that there were 'evil men' at work in this city. These were the individuals who had sold themselves over to Satan. Since they were cooperating with Satan, they should be seen as the powers and principalities – weapons at work to cause a standstill in the way of the gospel to fulfil the wish of their master, Satan.

Paul's view of the powers and principalities as weapons of spiritual warfare

The question can be asked, Who wages the war? Paul makes clear that these battles are championed by the enemies of the gospel.

Take the opposition that Paul met in Corinth, as reflected in the second letter to this church. For Paul, this was not a matter of physical encounter. It was a spiritual one. The enemies are those opponents seeking to destroy Paul. The sole objective was that by discrediting him they could ultimately discredit the gospel he had preached, which had resulted in the salvation of many converts. Paul records their accusation: 'For his letters, they say, are weighty and powerful, but his bodily presence is weak, and his speech contemptible' (2 Cor. 10:10). In the view of the opponents, if they succeeded in destroying Paul, then they would be able to draw back the new converts into their former ungodly life, inasmuch as that would have brought his message to a great disrepute. It is noteworthy then that Paul knew that 'Christian teachers and their teaching are subject to attack and distortion by the principalities and powers'.[6]

In the view of Paul, the attack from his opponents was not a mere physical battle. The powers and principalities were working through human agents. The work of Paul was causing great embarrassment in the kingdom of darkness. Hence a way must be found to bring it to a halt. The best way to do this was to incite some individuals to work at cross-purposes to the ministry of Paul. Paul knew that this was a battle to be fought. Thus he writes:

> But what I do, I will also continue to do, that I may cut off the opportunity from those who desire an opportunity to be regarded just as we are in the things of which they boast. For such are false apostles, deceitful workers, transforming themselves into apostle of Christ. And no wonder! For Satan himself transforms himself into an angel of light. Therefore it is no great thing if his ministers also transform themselves into minister of righteousness, whose end will be according to their works (2 Cor. 10:12-15).

The problem here is similar to the one in Galatia. There Paul identified the tactics of his opponents as trying to seduce his converts by placing the observance of the law as an important requirement for salvation. This was a clever way to cause derailment for Christians. The powers of darkness took up religious garb by way of religious observance of the law. But Paul responded swiftly, in the following words:

> O foolish Galatians! Who has bewitched you that you should not obey the truth, before whose eyes Jesus Christ was clearly portrayed among you as crucified? This only I want to learn from you: Did you receive the Spirit by the works of the law, or by the hearing of faith? Are you so foolish? Having begun in the Spirit, are you now being made perfect by the flesh? (Gal. 3:1-3).

Paul did not waste time to bring the judgement of God on these messengers of Satan. The right way he chose to do this was by placing them under the wrath of God, as he pronounced a curse upon them for their subtle work. In other words, whatever be the identity of such opponents of the gospel, they must be condemned. Hence he writes:

> But even if we, or an angel from heaven, preach any other gospel to you than what we have preached to you, let him be accursed. As we have said before, so now I say again, if anyone preaches any other gospel to you than what you have received, let him be accursed (Gal. 1:8-9).

Again the mention of 'angel' here as a vehicle for bringing the 'other gospel' to the Christians in Galatia is an obvious indication of the fact that not all angels exist to fulfil the good pleasure of God. Some of them are fallen creatures, who are consequently in the service of Satan. Indeed there were battles to be fought, and Paul was aware of this fact. He knew that they were spiritual battles that could not to be fought physically. Thus there was the need to approach these battles in the right attitude, 'lest Satan should take advantage of us; for we are not ignorant of his devices' (2 Cor. 2:11).

A few words used in 2 Corinthians 10:4-5 require further probing in order to give a clear picture of the text. If we understand these words properly, we will be able to enter into the thoughts of Paul and appreciate his understanding of the *powers* and *principalities* as weapons of spiritual warfare.

> For the weapons of our warfare are not carnal but mighty in God for pulling down strongholds, casting down arguments and every high thing that exalts itself against the knowledge of God, bringing every thought into captivity to the obedience of Christ (2 Cor. 10:4-5).

First, the word *stronghold*. A stronghold is *the power or co-ordinating point providing maximum security for effective sustenance of any given action*. The stronghold of Satan is the mind[7] of humans. This is the thought centre. That is where Satan aims at residing, or, shall we say, seeks to take over to establish his permanent reign. The purpose is to be able to suggest many options that are counter-productive to the Christian faith. He wants to do this to make believers restless and devoid of peace. If godly thoughts are banished from the heart, there cannot be peace. 'You will keep him in perfect peace, whose mind is stayed on You, because he trusts in You' (Isa. 26:3).

If the mind is filled with thoughts coming from the kingdom of darkness, believers will not be able to set their 'mind on things above' (Col. 3:2). Consequently, there will be a dethronement of *the only true God* from the same. It is in the mind that every form of argument rages. It is in the mind that the thought to exalt oneself above God emanates. What led to the fall of Satan from the outset also started from the mind: 'For you have said in your heart: I will ascend into heaven I will exalt my throne above the stars of God' (Isa. 14:13).[8] Satan should be constantly denied the opportunity of making our heart his stronghold. The best way to do this is to keep the word of God there, as underscored by the Psalmist: 'Your word I have hidden in my heart, that I may not sin against You' (Ps. 119:11).

Secondly is the word, *thought*. The power and strength of a man is best known in the expression of his thoughts. As a man is so he speaks. What a man does or acts out in the physical realm is the end product of the thoughts that have been conceived within him. Jesus brings out clearly the importance of the power of thoughts in His encounter with the Pharisees and the Lawyers as evidenced in the gospel:

> And when He had entered a house away from the crowd, His disciples asked Him concerning the parable. So He said to them, 'Are you thus without understanding also? Do you not perceive that whatever enters a man from outside cannot defile him, because it does not enter his heart but his stomach, and is eliminated, thus purifying all foods?' And He said, what comes out of a man, that defiles a man. For from within, out of the heart of men, proceed evil thoughts, adulteries, fornications, murders, thefts, covetousness, wickedness, deceit, licentiousness, an evil eye, blasphemy, pride, and foolishness. All these evil things come from within and defile a man (Mark 7:17-23).

What Satan does is to employ the services of his agents – the powers and principalities to saturate the thoughts of humans with many tempting suggestions, with the hope of a more rewarding life. In presenting these suggestions, Satan offers better options that should be more preferred than any pattern of life rooted in purity and godliness. This was what he did to the first Adam, and he fell (Gen. 3:1-6). Indeed, Satan comes 'to steal, and to kill and to destroy' (John 10:10a). In other words, when Satan takes over your thought life, he becomes the director of your life. This is the reason for Paul's admonition to the Galatians:

> Walk in the Spirit, and you shall not fulfil the lust of the flesh. For the flesh lusts against the Spirit, and the Spirit against the flesh; and these are contrary to one another; so that you do not do the things that you wish (Gal. 5:16-17).

Every suggestion coming from the devil is executed in the *flesh*. For Paul, *sin* is synonymous with 'the works of the flesh', which are manifested outwardly in concrete acts. However, what is later manifested in concrete outward acts first originates in the form of thoughts. Then the person begins to meditate on them, and if care is not taken, before such an individual knows what is happening, his thoughts have been taken over completely by the devil. The result is obvious, depending on the spirit (the force of darkness) that is at work. The works of the flesh are the manifestation of Satanic-controlled thoughts. They include 'adultery, fornication, uncleanness, licentiousness, idolatry, sorcery, hatred, contentions, jealousies, outburst of wrath, selfish ambitions, dissensions, heresies, envy, murders, drunkenness, revelries' (Gal. 5:19-21).

If 'disobedience' is another word for sin, and Paul says that the 'prince of the power of the air' is working 'in the sons of disobedience' (Eph. 2:2), then it can be postulated that Satan is behind every act of disobedience mentioned in Galatians 5:19-21. 'He who sins is of the devil, for the devil has sinned from the beginning' (1 John 3:8a). If the 'devil was a murderer from the beginning' (John 8:44), then Satan is behind murder. It is in the same way that Satan had prompted Herod to murder the innocent children (Matt. 2:16).[9] Thus, it is the power of darkness working behind every murderer, just as Satan rules the life of every adulterer. The point we are making here is that if sin is disobedience, and the Scripture makes it crystal clear that there is 'the spirit who now works in the sons of disobedience', then behind every manner of sin is the devil insofar as every demonic spirit is directly traceable to him.

Furthermore, this point is explicitly underscored in Paul's first letter to Timothy: 'Now the Spirit expressly says that in latter times some will depart from the faith, giving heed to deceiving spirits and doctrines of demons, speaking lies in hypocrisy' (1 Tim. 4:1-2). From the above, though the text says 'spirits,' it is apparent that forces of darkness are moving the hearts of people to promote the 'doctrines of demon,' as against the doctrines of God. This is the 'spirit of deceit' moving people to accept demonic teachings and to tell lies. Thus, as noted earlier, and in the light of the references above, it can be concluded that each of 'the works of the flesh' has a demonic spirit behind it as long as it is motivated by Satan, and therefore it is Satan that wages war against every human being with the suggestion to be disobedient to God.

Hence, believers' thoughts must be saturated with the word of God; otherwise forces of darkness will take over. There is a constant battle going on in the *thought compartment* of a believer. It is a battle between the Kingship of Jesus Christ and the lordship of Satan. Paul was aware of this, hence he declares, 'For the good that

I will to do, I do not do; but the evil I will not to do, that I practice...O wretched man that I am! Who will deliver me from this body of death?' (Rom. 7:19, 24). However, Paul's confession did not end on a gloomy note, for he concluded, 'I thank God – through Jesus Christ our Lord! (Rom. 7:25). In other words, forces of darkness may rage and fight, yet Christ has delivered believers from them.

One other point that we must mention is that the purpose for which the flesh wars against the Spirit is to ensure that Christians are brought back into the kingdom of darkness. If Satan succeeds in making Christians go back and take on board 'the works of the flesh' by capturing their thoughts through the operation of the powers and principalities, they 'will not inherit the kingdom of God' (Gal. 5:21b). If they miss the kingdom of God, that means eternal death. Simply put, the purpose for which 'the works of the flesh' exist is to bring humanity to death. That is the ultimate objective of Satan for fighting incessant battles against believers in the instrumentality of the powers and principalities. Michael Green has rightly pointed this out as he writes, 'Death is, accordingly, the supreme focus of these enemy forces. They smell of death. They revel in it. They spread it.'[10] Their ultimate focus is a reign of death, eternal damnation.

Down the ages, *corruption of the believers' thoughts* is one of the most effective methods the forces of darkness have been using to rend havoc on specially appointed servants of God. God specially appoints every believer for noble services. The most important of these services is the task of witnessing to the power of the gospel. But if Satan succeeds in corrupting the thoughts of a believer, then he has captured him. Take for example, king David. He first saturated the heart of David with the thoughts of adultery (2 Sam. 11:1-5), and later with the thoughts of murder (2 Sam. 11:6-27). The same thing goes for Ananias and Sapphira in the New Testament. Satan operated in their thoughts by moving their hearts to deceive the apostles. The result for them was instant death (Acts 5:1-11). He also tried the trick on the second Adam, Christ (Matt. 4:1-11), but Satan lost the battle to take hold of the thoughts of Christ. He could not control the thoughts of Christ, because Christ is the living word of God Himself, and He used the word to crush the devil.

Paul knew that if Satan can gain control of the heart of believers by occupying their thoughts with fabricated lies and present these to them as the truth (since he often shows himself as angel of light), they will be easily swept off the ground and fall. This is why it is important to know the truth of the word of God. For this reason, Jesus emphatically declared in the gospel, 'And you shall know the truth, and the truth shall make you free' (John 8:32).

Paul equally knows that if the centre of man's thought is filled with the right message, it will be difficult for the unseen forces of darkness to prevail against him. Thus he commands the Colossians, 'Let the word of Christ dwell in you richly in all wisdom...'(Col. 3:16).[11] What we are saying here is that if the thoughts of any Christian is rooted in the word of God, it will be difficult for the powers of darkness to play any trick on him. Like Jesus, whenever Satan appears with his suggestions, such a believer can confidently say, 'It is written.' But you can only say 'it is written' when you can recall in your thoughts what has been written.

Then comes the third word in 2 Corinthians 10:4-5 which is, *captivity*. In Paul's use of this word, there is a reversal of role. Paul here made a great acclamation, which is to bring into captivity every weapon Satan had used thus far. In a reversal of role, what Satan had done hitherto in the arena of spiritual warfare to take humans captive had been reversed. In other words, Satan had been brought in total subjection to the authority of Christ. If the thoughts of a believer had been previously taken over by Satan, now that the believer is 'in Christ,' those thoughts have been taken over by in obedience to Christ. Hence, Paul writes, 'Do you not know that to whom you present yourselves slaves to obey, you are that one's slave...?' (Rom. 6:16).

Paul was quite aware of the main goal of the devil, which is to bring back believers into captivity. It is a fierce battle for ownership.[12] Satan will not let go easily. Paul, as a pastor par excellence, was spiritually sensitive to the needs of his converts. He knew the danger of taking the gift of salvation for granted. Hence he wanted his converts to work out their salvation with fear and trembling (Phil. 2:12). The best way to do this was by unravelling before them the tricks of the devil who constantly wages unseen battles against them, in the instrumentality of the powers and principalities, seeking to pull them down into bondage.

In the view of Paul, Christians should not make the mistake of thinking that the battle is over. The words of O'Brien are helpful here:

> Although defeated foes the principalities and powers continue to exist, inimical to man and his interests. This is a reality even for the believer.... There will be no cessation of hostilities until our departure to be with Christ or his return, whichever is the sooner. Our struggle is not with human beings but with supernatural intelligences. Our enemies are not human but demonic, and they are powerful, wicked and cunning.[13]

Conclusion

In this chapter we have observed the following details. First, regarding the issue of whether or not Paul has any concrete idea of spiritual warfare, it is our contention that Paul knows that the Christian life is a complete warfare. In order to sustain his or her faith each believer must defend on a regular basis his or her new life; and this defence is not a matter of employing physical weapons since the battle is not fought physically.

Secondly, the opponents of Paul were enemies of the gospel manifesting their wicked acts through religious and civil institutions (Acts 16:16-24), which aimed at thwarting the plan of God to bring salvation. Yet, Paul knew that they were not on their own accord responsible for their actions; rather whatever they did was the outward expression of that which was happening in the kingdom of darkness, of which Satan is the head (Acts 19:26-27).

5

The Cross of Christ as the Defeat of the Powers and Principalities

In this chapter our focus will be on the cross of Christ as God's chosen way for completely rescuing humanity from the horrendous attacks of the powers and principalities in the ongoing spiritual warfare. Satan and his cohorts may be powerful and wicked, but they are not in any way omnipotent. In other words, the forces of the dark kingdom, namely the powers and principalities, should not be seen as uncontrollable or invincible. It is important to know that Satan has been vested with great power, but only to the degree that God allows him to operate. In other words, Satan has a limited power. This is evident in Scripture:

> Then the LORD said to Satan, 'Have you considered My servant Job, that there is none like him on the earth, a blameless and upright man, one who fears God and shuns evil?' So Satan answered the LORD and said, 'Does Job fear God for nothing? Have You not made a hedge around him, around his household, and around all that he has on every side? You have blessed the work of his hands, and his possessions have increased in the land. But now, stretch out Your hand and touch all that he has, and he will surely curse You to your face!' So the LORD said to Satan, 'Behold, all that he has is in your power; only do not lay a hand on his person' (Job 1:8-12 cf. 2:3-6).

These verses make it clear that it was God who determined the extent to which Satan should afflict Job. Hence Satan is not the *Almighty*. His authority, or rather his power, is a subjugated one. This point is clearly made by Michael Green as he underscores the limitation of the power of Satan, 'His power, though great, is limited by God's *fiat*. He is a creature and is ultimately subject to God's authority.'[1]

Satan does not mean well for humanity. If there is anything that he does, it is to ensure that humanity is doomed eternally. In his encounter with the *first Adam* in the Garden of Eden (Gen. 3), Satan succeeded in turning man's heart away from God to follow his own perverted ways. He tried to tempt the *second Adam* (Luke 4:1-12), with a view to frustrating God's plan of redemption for mankind, but he failed. However, he did not easily give up on Christ (Luke 4:13), insofar as he sought another opportunity to carry out his onslaught against Him. Indeed, the battle led to the cruel and ignominious death of Christ on the cross at Calvary. Yes, it is in this sense that Calvary became the place where Satan and his kingdom were ultimately destroyed. Green brings out this point succinctly: 'Satan has lain under judgement since Eden. The judgement was implemented on Calvary. The sentence passed on Satan in Genesis 3 has been executed. Strong man that he is, he has been dispossessed and bound by the Stronger than the strong, Jesus himself (Mark 3:27).'[2]

It is not our intention here to repeat what we have already discussed in chapter 3. Nevertheless, a recapitulation of a few points made there is helpful for our present discussion. If Paul were to be around today and we should ask him the question, 'who crucified Jesus?' I believe Paul would neither regard the duo of Caiaphas and Pilate (who were the official representatives of the state and religion) nor the Jewish mob (the Pharisees, the Sadducees, the Scribes and the entire crowd) as those who crucified Jesus. Instead, for Paul these individuals were mere weaponries of the kingdom of darkness. In them the kingdom of darkness found ready instruments to achieve its goal of crucifying the King of glory.

But herein lies the victory of the cross over the kingdom of darkness, over the powers and principalities. In recognition of this defeat, Paul writes: 'But we speak the wisdom of God in a mystery, the hidden wisdom which God ordained before the ages for our glory, which none of the rulers of this age knew; for had they known, they would not have crucified the Lord of glory' (1 Cor. 2:7-8).

The life and ministry of Christ in perspective
The events of the crucifixion and resurrection of Jesus Christ should be seen as the grand finale of His life and ministry. From the birth

of Christ, 'the rulers of this world' knew that the judgment of God had come upon their tyrannical government. While it could be argued that Jesus did not receive any official recognition until his baptism at River Jordan (Matt. 3:17) when he began his public ministry, yet from the moment of his birth the kingdom of darkness had known that the Seed of the woman who would bruise the head of the serpent had been born. Therefore, efforts had to be made to prevent Christ from establishing and exercising the ultimate authority of the Father. For the hosts of darkness this newly born 'King,' whose reign or Kingdom will have no end, must be killed. This informed the rearing up of their heads in the person of king Herod at the birth of Christ:

> Now after Jesus was born in Bethlehem of Judea in the days of Herod the king, behold, wise men from the East came to Jerusalem, saying where is He who has been born King of the Jews? For we have seen His star in the East and have come to worship Him. When Herod the king heard these things, he was troubled, and all Jerusalem with him. And when he had gathered all the chief priests and scribes of the people together, he inquired of them where the Christ was to be born. So they said unto him, in Bethlehem of Judea.... Then Herod, when he had secretly called the wise men, determined from them what time the star appeared. And he sent them to Bethlehem and said, 'Go and search diligently for the young Child, and when you have found Him, bring back word to me, that I may come and worship Him also'.... Then Herod, when he saw that he was deceived by the wise men, was exceedingly angry, and he sent forth and put to death all the male children who were in Bethlehem and in all its districts, from two years old and under, according to the time which he had determined from the wise men (Matt. 2:1-5, 7-8,16).

While on the one hand Herod had given the wise men the impression of a genuine desire to worship the newly born King, on the other hand his desire was to kill Jesus Christ because he saw Him as a threat to his own ungodly kingship and authority. This explains why Herod and all Jerusalem were 'troubled' at the news of the birth of Christ. As noted by Richard Niswonger, 'Herod's order to the Magi to return after they had found the Child so that he might worship him reveals the cunning of a king who was ever alert to any political winds that might affect his control of the throne.'[3]

We see the wickedness of the powers and principalities at work here. Satan had moved the heart of Herod to 'put to death all the male children who were in Bethlehem and in all its districts, from two years old and under, according to the time which he had determined from the wise men' (Matt. 2:16). While it was not explicit from the passage that Satan had entered into Herod[4] to perpetrate the cruel act, yet it is apparent that he was not acting on his own, but that demonic spirits had taken possession of him, causing him to attempt to kill Christ. Herod displayed his ignorance of the eternal plan of God as prophesied by Isaiah: 'For unto us a Child is born, unto us a Son is given; and the government will be upon His shoulder.... Of the increase of His government and peace there will be no end' (Isa. 9:6-7). In other words, Herod, a ready tool in the hands of Satan, cannot undo what God had ordained from the beginning in making provision to liberate humanity through His Son.

The ministry of Christ was the full manifestation of the arrival of the Kingdom of God, which has been established not only to overshadow, but also to overthrow the kingdom of darkness. Christ has come to bind the strong man, so that He can raid his house. Jesus went about healing those who had been bound by the spirits of infirmities and casting out demons and restoring wholeness to people. The powers were forced to acknowledge Christ's supremacy over them as they cry, 'Let us alone! What have we to do with You, Jesus of Nazareth? Did You come to destroy us? I know who You are – the Holy One of God!' (Mark 1:24).

Jesus' ministry undoubtedly sets Him in open confrontation with the various religious institutions of His day. The Pharisees, the Sadducees and the Scribes were always querying His right to heal and set people free, simply because such acts of mercy were done on the Sabbath (Mark 3:1-6) or because He was interacting with those regarded as the rejects and outcasts of the society (Luke 19:10). The only strategy readily available to Satan was to move the hearts of the religious and civil authorities of Jesus' day to kill Him. 'Then the Pharisees went out and immediately plotted with the Herodians against Him, how they might destroy Him' (Mark 3:6). The reason for such plots was because Jesus was snatching the victims of the kingdom of darkness from the clusters of Satan.

The mystery of the cross in Paul's thought

God had a reason for sending Christ to the world (John 3:16). In agreement with the Father's will, Christ also knew the purpose for which He came to the world since He clearly declared, 'For even the Son of Man did not come to be served, but to serve, and to give His life a ransom for many' (Mark 10:45). While there had been an unmistakable demonstration of the superiority of the Kingdom of God over the kingdom of Satan in the life and ministry of Christ, yet the final blow had not been dealt on the powers of Satan. This is to be demonstrated in the death and resurrection of Christ. Herein lies the mystery that Paul writes about in 1 Corinthians 2:7: 'But we speak the wisdom of God in a *mystery*, the hidden wisdom which God ordained before the ages for our glory.'

Mystery, in this context, does not refer to the esoteric religions of the Graeco-Roman world; rather it refers to God's appointed way of saving humanity. As noted by Gordon Fee, 'the term "mystery" ordinarily refers to something formerly hidden in God from *all* human eyes but now revealed in history through Christ and made understandable to his people through the Spirit.'[5] Leon Morris also writes: 'It [mystery] signifies a secret which man is wholly unable to penetrate.... It is revealed to believers, but it is not a matter of common knowledge among the sons of men. It remains hidden from unbelievers.'[6] This mystery was too difficult for the demonic institutions that crucified Christ to unravel.

Indeed, how would the rulers of the world understand this great mystery that their defeat lay in the crucifixion of Christ on the cross? God had kept it from them so that they could be part of the means God had chosen to complete His eternal plan of salvation for mankind (atonement for their sin in the death of Christ, John 1:29). Also by this means God had chosen to bring judgement upon the forces of darkness by rendering them impotent eternally (1 John 3:8b, cf. John 12:31). In other words, the fierce antagonism of the powers of darkness 'becomes precisely the vehicle for world redemption: of this the Cross itself is the supreme illustration.'[7]

If there is any passage that brings out the most inclusive nature of Satan's doom, it is Colossians 2:14-15, where Paul writes: '...having wiped out the handwriting of requirements that was against us, which was contrary to us. And He has taken it out of the way, having nailed it to the cross. Having disarmed principalities and powers, He made a public spectacle of them, triumphing over them in it.'

Bearing in mind our earlier discussion in chapter 4 that behind every sin is the demonic spirit,[8] thus it becomes apparent that the spirit of heresy had taken possession of some of the Colossians so that they were beginning to go back to their old sinful life. If there is any thing that Paul did on a regular basis among his converts, it was to remind them of the sufficiency of the death and resurrection of Christ as the truth they needed to maintain them to the end of their Christian race.

The heresy among the Colossians was 'probably a Phrygian development in which a local variety of Judaism had been fused with philosophy of non-Jewish origin – an early and simple form of gnosticism.... In this heresy a special place was apparently given to angels, as agents both in creation and in the giving of the law.'[9] Special attention was given to the angelic beings believing them to have taken active part in the creation of man. This was based on Genesis 1:26 ('Let *us* make man') and Genesis 3:22 ('the man has become like one of *us*').

The faith of the Colossians was certainly on the downward trend. Hence, according to Macgregor, 'The very crux of the Colossians heresy is that these folk are giving to the *stoicheia* [elemental spirits], as mediators between God and man, the place which can belong only to Christ.'[10] This was a great challenge to the integrity of God and the truth of the gospel that acknowledges Jesus Christ as the sole creative Power of God.

The heretical teachers (the agents of the dark kingdom) wanted believers in Colossae to disbelieve the gospel previously preached to them. These believers had been taught that Jesus Christ is the fullness of God, and that in Him everything holds together. If the heretics could succeed in giving prominence to angelic beings as the vehicles of creation, then Jesus could not be the sole Saviour of mankind. The angelic beings then must be operating not only at a par with Christ, but also far above Him.

The connection of the angelic beings with 'the law' in the Colossian heresy could probably be understood in the light of Paul's usage of 'elemental beings' in Galatians 4:3 and 9, as if the powers and principalities were behind the giving and observance of the legalistic requirements of the law. Commenting on the roles the angels had played in the lives of the Colossians before their conversion experience, N.T. Wright states:

> The point he [Paul] wishes to make is that the Colossians had formerly been under the domination of these powers, (a) because they were members of pagan society and its religions, and (b) because the angels who had given the Law thus functioned as guardians, keeping Gentiles excluded from the family of God.[11]

The main goal of these heretical teachers was to devalue the centrality of Christ as the only means of fellowship with God. If they succeeded in attributing a special importance to the angels, it would mean that communion with God would only be possible with God via these angels. In this respect, Bruce has noted:

> In the Colossian heresy the keeping of the law was regarded as a tribute of obedience due to those angels, and the breaking of the law incurred their displeasure and brought the law-breaker into debt and bondage to them. Hence they must be placated not only by legal observances of traditional Judaism but in addition by a rigorous asceticism.[12]

There is no doubt that the kingdom of darkness was at work operating through its agents in the garb of false teachers. For Paul, such teachings required immediate repudiation, and presenting the pre-eminence of Christ and the fullness of His work was the way to do it. Stewart's observation rightly fits in here:

> Thus the pre-existence of Christ means that He was before the angelic rulers, before creation itself: 'in Him all things were created', writes

Paul to the Colossians, and specifically mentions the [archai] and [echousiai] which, casting off their original allegiance, revolted into demonism. Having been created 'in Him' they are essentially subject powers.[13]

For Paul, realising the authority and pre-eminence of Christ is all that the Colossians required to keep their spiritual bearing in the right perspective. If believers are already in Christ, they need not seek access into the presence of God through any angelic beings. If Jesus Christ is the 'power and wisdom of God' (1 Cor. 1:24), and believers are already living in Him, they need no specially revealed esoteric knowledge from the angelic beings to know the mind of God and fellowship with Him. More importantly this fact must be presented in the defeat of the principalities and powers and their subjugation to the authority of Christ.

The crucifixion of Christ was an epoch-making event. On the one hand, it achieved the redemption of man; and on the other hand, it signalled the defeat of the powers and principalities. The fulfilment of the wish of the powers and principalities to see Christ crucified also meant their own complete destruction. In other words, 'The very instrument of disgrace and death by which the hostile forces thought they had him in their grasp and had conquered him forever was turned by him into the instrument of their defeat and disablement....Whatever power they once exercised, they are now the "weak and beggarly elemental forces" that Paul declares them to be in Gal. 4:9.'[14]

The relevance of Colossians 2:15 to Paul's argument

In what way are we to understand that, by crucifying Christ in their ignorance, the powers and principalities have been dealt a death blow on their kingdom? The answer is detailed in Colossians 2:15: 'Having disarmed principalities and powers, He made a public spectacle of them, triumphing over them in it.' There are three points to note for our understanding of how the cross of Christ executed defeat on the kingdom of darkness.

First is the *disarmament* of the principalities and powers. How did Christ do this? He did this by voluntarily giving Himself to be nailed to the cross to fulfil in all its ramifications the demands of the law. In His death, Christ who knew no sin was made sin and died an accursed death on the cross! This is the sense in which He is the end of the law (Rom. 10:4). The law is given to show the magnitude of sin (Rom. 3:20b), and when sin is fully grown, it results in death (Rom. 6:23a). The law was only an effective document in taking the records of the misdeeds of mankind before God. This is the sense in which 'the letter kills' (2 Cor. 3:6), since there are demonic spirits always to accuse the transgressor for violating the requirement of the law. Christ had disarmed this document and all the forces of darkness operating behind it by nailing them to the cross. Hence, in the view of Bruce, 'It might even be said that he took the document, ordinances and all and nailed it to his cross as an act of defiance in the face of those blackmailing powers that were holding it over men and women in order to command their allegiance.'[15]

In His death on the cross, Christ liberated humanity from the tyrannical rule of the principalities and powers. He broke the stronghold of Satan. Just as the entrance of sin into the world had a universal effect, so also the victory that Jesus won over the powers of darkness has cosmic effects. Although the final redemption of believers is at the parousia, we must not be ignorant of the effect of the cross of Christ over the powers of darkness in the present age – the powers and principalities have been rendered inoperative. To use the words of Paul 'the rulers of this age' have come 'to nothing' (1 Cor. 2:6). Though they exist, in the real sense of it they are powerless. Indeed, they have been disarmed. They can no longer hold humans to ransom.

The second point to consider is the fact that Christ has *made a public spectacle of them* – the powers and principalities. Other versions of the Bible render the same text, 'He made an open show of them,' or 'He made a public exhibition of them.' What does it mean to make an open show or a public exhibition of something? It means the bringing out of the emptiness of a particular thing, or the extent of the strength of that thing. Thus in making a public spectacle of the powers of darkness, Christ affirmed in an uncompromising way the reality that, 'All authority has been given to Me in heaven and on earth' (Matt. 28:18). In making a public spectacle of the powers of Satan, Jesus Christ has declared openly how powerless is the 'powerful Satan'.

In His once and for all declaration on the cross at Calvary that 'It is finished' (John 19:30), Jesus Christ shows the emptiness of the boasting of Satan who has relentlessly claimed to be in charge of the *authority* and *glory* of *the kingdoms of this world* (Luke 4:5-6). In his defeat on the cross at Calvary, Satan has been brought to his knees to acknowledge his status as a liar. All authority and the glory of this world do not belong to him, but rather to God, insofar as 'the earth is the LORD's, and all its fullness' (Ps. 24:1). The only person to whom God has given this authority is His Son Jesus Christ, whom He has appointed to be the judge of the whole world (John 5:22). He has established firmly His authority, so much so that the principalities and powers that were the enemies of the Son of God have now become His footstool (Heb. 1:13).

The third point is the fact that Christ has *triumphed over them in it.* Yes, He triumphed over the principalities and powers in His death on the cross. He had taken them captive. The Stronger has completely bound the 'strong man'. The point of emphasis here is that the cross of Christ is what brought about the abrogation of the powers of the kingdom of darkness. This 'triumph' is to be explained in the context of the resurrection of Jesus Christ. The empty tomb is what proved the powers of darkness wrong. The 'rulers of this age' had thought they had destroyed the Son of God. No wonder there was no objection from Pilate when Joseph of Aramathea came for the body of Christ to be buried in his tomb.

However, the rulers got the great shock of their lives when they received the news of the resurrection of Christ. While for the believers this was the culmination of the good news that started on Good Friday at Calvary, for 'the rulers of this age', it was a bad news for them. The Scripture bears witness:

> Now while they were going, behold, some of the guard came into the city and reported to the chief priests all the things that had happened. When they had assembled with the elders and taken counsel, they gave a large sum of money to the soldiers, saying, 'Tell them, His disciples came at night and stole Him away while we slept. And if this comes to the governor's ears, we will appease him and make you

secure. So they took the money and did as they were instructed (Matt. 28:11-15a).

Satan was still at work, even at the resurrection of Christ, by putting in them a lying spirit (since he is the father of all liars). But it was too late for the enemy. The bribe offered and received by all the forces of darkness operating in the chief priests and the soldiers could not bring Christ back to the grave. Christ has been resurrected. He could not be bound by the power of death. Christ has triumphed over all the lies and bribery of the devil. He has triumphed over all the wickedness of the devil. He had triumphed over the pride of the devil. Yes, in all its ramifications, the crucified and resurrected Christ *triumphed over them all in it*. Thus, in the resurrection of Christ, Paul demonstrates clearly that God has shown the

> Exceeding greatness of His power toward us who believe, according to the working of His mighty power which He worked in Christ when He raised Him from the dead and seated Him at His right hand in the heavenly places, far above all principality and power and might and dominion, and every name that is named, not only in this age but also in that which is to come. And He put all things under His feet, and gave Him to be head over all things to the church, which is His body, the fullness, of Him who fills all in all (Eph. 1:19-23).

In other words, for Paul, there is no way the heretical teachers should draw back the Colossian Christians to believe that the principalities and powers in the garb of angelic beings were superior to Jesus Christ. He is the author and finisher of the believer's faith. In Him consists the fullness of everything, whether in heaven or on the earth. He has won absolute victory over the powers of darkness. Yes, in His death and resurrection Christ had vanquished them.

Conclusion

As we conclude this chapter, it is important to restate our major point, that the death of Christ on the cross was the decisive event in the final conquest of the powers of darkness, and the release of victory to believers. The cross was, and is still, a great mystery for the kingdom of darkness. The nailing of Christ to the cross epitomises cruelty of the highest order. The cross was the converging point for the demonic religious, political and social institutions of Jesus' time. In the crucifixion of Christ, the powers and principalities were exhibiting their wickedness in these institutions.

On the one hand, these demonic institutions might seem to have triumphed in crucifying Christ, but on the other hand for God and His Christ the death on the cross at Calvary became the divinely appointed way to inflict final destructive blow on these seeming powers. God passed on the demonic kingdom the eternal judgment of defeat. As clearly expressed by Stewart:

> When Jesus became obedient unto death, even the death of the cross, He did it in the confidence that in this final act the dark powers would overreach themselves and so be finished for ever: had they known that, Paul suggests, they would never have done it. But this was the will of Jesus in His death.[16]

Therefore while the rulers of this world thought that they were terminating the ministry of Christ with His crucifixion on the cross, they were actually inflicting eternal defeat on their ungodly powers. If the principalities and powers had known that the death of Christ on the cross was God's appointed way to declare final doom on the kingdom of darkness, these rulers would have avoided the way of the cross.

6

African Concept of Spiritual Warfare and the Use of the Powers as Weapons of Spiritual Warfare

Introduction

The concept of spiritual warfare in African culture is a real phenomenon that goes beyond ordinary imagination. It is important from the outset to identify the limit of our task in the present chapter. We shall focus on Yorubaland, which is an area in Nigeria occupied by the Yoruba-speaking peoples. The choice of Yorubaland is motivated by the fact that the author comes from this part of Nigeria.

The name 'Yoruba' is a designation commonly used to cover a large ethnic group in Nigeria numbering several millions of people who are united more by a common language (*Yoruba*)[1] and culture rather than by any political inclinations. These people have never constituted a single political party or formed a unitary nation-state, but instead their ethnic solidarity can be traced to the traditions of a common origin in the town of Ile-Ife in Osun state.[2]

The unity of the Yoruba race is due to a common historical experience facilitated by social and geographical mobility, which is evident in their increased degree of cultural and linguistic uniformity.[3] While the Yoruba race is scattered all over the world,[4] their homeland is mainly in the South Western part of Nigeria, which includes the present day states of Lagos, Ogun, Oyo, Ondo, Osun and Ekiti.[5] In effect, Yorubaland is synonymous with the south-western part of Nigeria.

It is our aim to demonstrate that the African concept of spiritual warfare as exemplified among the Yoruba replicates the experience of the Ephesians of Paul's day. Therefore Paul's admonition in Ephesians 6:10-12 is as relevant to African Christians in contemporary society as it was to the Ephesians of the first century. Our discussion will be approached from two angles. First, we shall examine briefly the African concept of spiritual warfare, noting the way it differs from Paul's concept of spiritual warfare; and secondly we shall look at the weapons at the disposal of Africans in the events of spiritual warfare. Our discussion will be concluded by demonstrating the futility of the African weapons of spiritual warfare, since they are incapable of true deliverance from the forces of darkness.

African concept of spiritual warfare: the Yoruba experience
The concept of spiritual warfare among the Yoruba to a great extent cannot be compared to Paul's concept of spiritual warfare. This is simply because what the various individuals are contending with is not the 'faith which was once for all delivered to' all believers who are 'in Christ' as the case was in Jude 3 and 2 Corinthians 5:17 respectively. Rather, the essence of spiritual warfare is to be able to keep at bay the enemies who are fighting both seen and unseen battles night and day.

These battles have nothing to do primarily with the integrity of the new life 'in Christ', because those who are engaged in this form of spiritual warfare can be described mainly as people 'without Christ, being aliens from the commonwealth of Israel [Christians] and strangers from the covenant of promise,' to use the words of Ephesians 2:12. Such battles could either be as a result of the success of an individual financially, educationally, matrimonially, professionally or fame. There is no ceasefire in this battle, even when asleep.

The forces of darkness require no special reasons before they attack. They operate at will to rend havoc on their victims. The victim does not even know where the attack is coming from or who is attacking. The offence may not be at all serious – a minor disagreement over a trivial issue is enough to incur the wrath of the attacker. But because the 'strong man' has demonic power at his disposal, he seeks to humiliate his victim – to make him unhappy, kill his children, break his marriage or destroy his business. In other words, you need not be an offender to be targeted by the opposing forces. The fact that a person is successful in life is enough to incur the wrath of wicked people. Adedeji writes:

Our environment [in Africa] suggests to us that there are foes everywhere and that you do not necessarily have to have offended people before they seek to harm you. There are people who take delight in testing their powers on others. This makes people justify those who seek to possess some powers for defensive purposes. They would not go anywhere until they are well fortified against likely attacks.[6]

People go about in suspicion of whether or not they are being targeted for a wicked act. A non-Christian African is very sensitive to the harm, misfortune or calamities unseen powers could bring on him. Thus he is very conscious of how he interacts in public. He will neither sit down anywhere, nor just eat anyhow. These are important acts with serious consequences for him. Again, Adedeji writes:

An African who is not a Christian does not just sit anywhere at a gathering. He would first try to ascertain if the person sitting next to him has stronger powers than him. If he does, the chances are there that he would refuse the seat even when ushers offer it, for fear of losing his own powers to the stronger man. When this happens, he has to pay much more to receive the demons into his life.[7]

Even though we have suggested that one's spiritual stance is not a major cause for attack from the African perspective, yet it could be in specific instances. When members of different groups perpetrate evil acts in the community, forces of darkness may not be angry with them. However, when such persons are changed spiritually and translated from the kingdom of darkness to that of light (2 Cor. 5:17), there would be serious opposition from those in the group to which they once belonged. Renouncing membership of a society or religious group is regarded as a breach of covenant or a betrayal of faith. Hence, such an act would be seen as an attempt to expose the secrets of the former group. What usually follows is the aggressive and intense persecution of the one-time members. The experience of an evangelist, Joshua Balogun, substantiates this claim. In his testimony he described how after his conversion he was abducted by the members of the Islamic group to which he had belonged previously:

As I was going along a major road one day in Lagos, a Peugeot 505 car parked by my side and the two men inside asked me, 'Alhaji, where are you going?' And I told them that I was going to Oyingbo, and from Oyingbo to Apapa Road. They said that they were going to Ijora. 'Come in, we would give you a lift.' Unaware of their plan, as soon as I entered ointment was rubbed into my eyes which made me lose my sight temporarily; and I was carried away to an unknown destination. It was in the process of being driven away that I heard one of them saying, 'You think you can run away from us. You want to turn our mosque into a church. You can go now and let us see how you would do it.' That was when I knew that these people were Muslims. Later they took me into particular bush and forced me into an already prepared iron cage that was short of my full length, padlocked it and left me to die in anguish. However, in the same manner that the angel of the Lord came and rescued Peter from the prison, I was rescued after seven days. Truly Christ is the same yesterday, today and forever.[8]

In physical warfare, weapons such as guns, cutlasses or machetes are used freely, and in the case of any casualties the accused person can be arrested and tried in the law court. But in the case of spiritual warfare, invisible weapons are used, resulting in the sudden death of the victims. The architects of such evil acts are not easily apprehended because their satanic acts have been carried out in the spirit world.

Spiritual warfare for an African is in various degrees. It touches on anything that can inhibit personal fulfilment and joy. Somebody who was once rich and enjoyed the good company of the affluent in the society can be targeted and rendered poor and miserable. In fact, wealth or good living can become a thing of the past for such a man who had once lived a fulfilled life. A pertinent case in this connection is that of a fifteen-year old girl whose story was reported in *Tell Magazine*, under the caption, 'Exploits of the Exorcist.' Here is the confession of Oluponna Alaba, a teenager who used her satanic power to impoverish her mother in addition to the disaster she had inflicted on her father. This girl comes from Ikere-Ekiti, Ekiti State, Nigeria:

Claimed to possess three black birds within her. Armed with her evil power, she claimed to have caused her father, who was also present at the vigil [where the confession was made], to go blind. How? She did this by pointing, as instructed, a palm kernel given to her by a fellow witch, in the direction of her father's eyes. It was punishment, she said, for her father who was accused of always intruding into other people's affairs. Besides, Oluponna also claimed to have given the 'calabash of the unknown' to her mother which has ruined her booming business, leaving her with nothing but poverty. According to her, she attends meetings with other witches at their coven under a tree at Ikere-Ekiti.[9]

Just as Paul writes to the Ephesians that their spiritual warfare is not with *flesh* and *blood*, but 'against principalities, against powers, against the rulers of the darkness of this age, against spiritual hosts of wickedness in the heavenly places' (Eph. 6:12), so also from the African perspective spiritual warfare has the same implications. In other words, the battle is not between two opponents engaged in a physical combat. The warfare is dangerous in the sense that the victim does not know where the offensive weapons are coming from, and neither does he know who are behind such terrible acts. There are flying arrows by day and great terrors by night (Ps. 91:5). The best an individual can do is to fortify himself with weapons he believes are strong enough to offer protection in case of attack by enemies.

Weapons of spiritual warfare among the Yoruba

To begin with, we need to remind ourselves of what we mean by the *powers*.[10] By that term we mean the various methods employed by the Yoruba to defend themselves against the onslaught of enemies or to attack targeted victims. These *powers* which they see as *weapons of their spiritual warfare* are to be understood from Paul's perspective of 'the principalities, powers, the rulers of the darkness of this age, and spiritual hosts of wickedness in the heavenly places' (Eph. 6:12). These become operational through different media.

In this respect, objects play significant roles as media for the release of *powers* for spiritual warfare. However, it should be borne in mind that these objects are of no consequence apart from spirits inhabiting them. These demonic spirits have elevated them to the status of extraordinary objects, making them the weaponries of the kingdom of darkness. However, because of cultural differences, and as a matter of ignorance, there is the tendency for those in the western world to dismiss as mythological and mere vestiges of a primitive culture the use of objects as channels for the release of powers by the forces of darkness to engage in spiritual warfare.

Nevertheless, whether such people believe in this kind of transfer of power or not, it is very real in the spirit world. It does not require any scientific proof to validate this kind of operation. Scepticism cannot invalidate its potency. Experience is the best teacher! Timmons, a white missionary from North America, remarks in this direction:

> For example, because we do not see many people using charms here in the United States, we do not understand what they are and how they work or function. We are spiritually dense and thus ask the wrong questions. How can a charm, for example, attract people to my place of business? How can a charm cause me to become wealthy? How does one cause death for my enemies? We fail to understand because we focus on the physical aspects of the charm and fail to see the underlying spiritual forces behind the operation of that charm. That is where the power is and not in the charm itself. A mirror of itself has no power. A waistband of itself has no power. A thread of cloth of itself has no power. A ring of itself has no power. Therefore, we tend to disbelieve the truth because we think, 'How can a ring cause people to go blind?' But the truth of the matter is, it is not the ring, but rather the demon forces operating through that object [that make these objects as mentioned above weaponries in the hands of the agents of Satan].[11]

There is no argument about the fact that the use of the powers is as old as the cultures of many African communities. This is equally true with special reference to the Yoruba people. Nearly every town in Yorubaland has behind it a record of history that can be best explained from the perspective of various wars fought in the time past to gain victory over their enemies or to escape from within the reach of their enemies.[12]

In every tribe or ethnic group, heroes emerged during the time of war who were known for their extraordinary courage and influence, not just because of their natural strength but more importantly for their use of various supernatural powers which accounted for victories over the opposing forces.

In the process of fighting such wars, while the use of physical weapons such as cutlasses, guns, and other materials was in great demand, people came to realise that the use of spiritual powers was much more effective. Therefore, even in the present day, there are special powers attributed to certain local heroes and features in many towns in Yorubaland that were instrumental for gaining victories over enemies in the past. These have been deified as objects to be venerated. Take for instance, *Olumo* Rock in Abeokuta, *Oranmiyan* Staff in Ile-Ife, *Osun* River in Osogbo and *Orosun* Hill in Idanre. The use of the powers; be it good or bad, depends on a single motif – the quest for exercise of authority over other people, the wish to be above everybody.

We shall look at the *powers* as spiritual weapons from four perspectives, highlighting in each case how they are used in the battle arena. While this broad classification is desirable, it must be noted that it will not be a watertight classification. Occasionally, there may be an overlap. Whatever happens, we will ensure that enough justification is given to every point discussed for the avoidance of any unnecessary repetition. The four perspectives are the practice of witchcraft, the use of magic, the use of charms, and enlistment in the membership of secret cults.

Closely connected to the operation of each of these weapons is 'the use of words' – *incantations*. Since the power of the spoken word, as evident in the use of incantation, is intrinsically bound with each of the classifications, we have hesitated to treat it in isolation.

The practice of witchcraft

The use of the power of witchcraft,[13] according to the beneficiaries, can either be positive or negative, depending on the circumstances. Witchcraft can be classified into three broad categories: white, black or red witchcraft. Each of these functions in accordance with the nature of operation carried out in the kingdom of darkness. For instance, it is believed that white witchcraft is useful for good work.

In this case the individuals possessed by the power of white witchcraft use the powers to protect themselves, their children or business against any external invasion. However, this is still a kingdom divided against itself, insofar as the powers of a stronger demon is used to fight weaker demonic spirits.[14] Black witchcraft is noted for perpetrating evil in all its ramifications. Its operations are without any mercy. Red witchcraft is associated with blood shedding and sucking. The African warriors depend more on this in the time of physical battles. This group of witchcraft is behind terrible communal conflicts and clashes in some certain geographical locations. It is the most wicked of all the three categories, and very ruthless in its operations. The personal confession of Florence Olayemi, a 38-year old woman whose case was reported in the *Tell Magazine*, substantiates this claim. According to Florence Olayemi:

> She possesses evil birds – two black and one red – which empower her to suck blood and eat the flesh of human beings. Florence, who claimed to be the chief caterer '*Alase*' in her group, said her own delicacy is the thigh of human beings.[15]

In spiritual warfare, activities of witches and wizards are of great significance. They are effective weaponries in the dark kingdom. Indeed, their operation is highly spiritual since they are in many ways invisible. They attack by the use of spirits and forces received from the kingdom of darkness in such a way that their victims are kept in the dark about all the havocs they have done, the ones they are doing; or what they will do in the very near future. Generally, witches and wizards whether *white*, *black* or *red* are merciless in their operations. Take the confession of Lola Adebayo, a twelve-year-old girl. In her confession she claimed

> to have possessed three red evil birds with which she claimed to have paralysed her younger sister and made her an imbecile. How on earth could she have done that? Well, she told the congregation [gathered at St. Michael's United Evangelical Miracle Church, Aramoko-Ekiti, Ekiti State, Nigeria] that she hid her brain inside a tree. Why? So that her parents would give attention to only her.[16]

From the above, it is obvious that wicked activities of witches and wizards are in different degrees. They are able to inflict diseases on their victims, cause accidents during journey, remove joy and prosperity from matrimonial homes, cause chaos among the best of friends, and even move two communities to engage in physical battles for various reasons. Therefore it is very dangerous to be an unbeliever!

Witches and wizards are nocturnal spirits, and so the best time for their operation is at night, mainly between the hours of midnight and 3 a.m. The method of their operation is by turning themselves into creatures such as bats, owls, snakes, rats, birds of different forms, cats and other carnivorous animals.[17] Essentially to the non-initiate, during the hours of operation, witches and wizards still remain as normal human beings on their beds, giving the impression that they are ordinarily asleep. But in reality, they have travelled far and extensively into the world of the spirits. There is no manner of restriction for them to get at their victims. This is what made them spirit-beings. One of the effective media of their operation is in the dream arena.

By dreams, what we are suggesting is satanic dreams. Satanic dreams involve spiritual warfare between two opposing parties. Since the forces of darkness are merciless, they cannot be pacified, appeased or placated. There is no ceasefire in this form of spiritual warfare. The battle is ongoing every moment, both night and day, until there is the death of the weaker opponent. Simply put, in this battle it is the survival of the fittest.

Dreams are thoughts visualised in sleep. What is thought of in the day is brought into the unconscious mind in sleep (Eccl. 5:3). The soul brings to remembrance what the spirit has engaged in the unconscious state. In other words, while the body is inactive at sleep, both spirit and soul are actively engaged, and there is intra-communication. They are sending out signals and receiving messages, whether positive or negative. Some of the physical wounds in real life situations are inflicted in the dream arena. In other words, the agents of darkness in the dream arena could have deposited in the lives of their victims most of the unpleasant experiences of real life they are battling with.

In dreams, the person planning the mischievous acts brings his action to bear on the life of his victim by way of trying to take life out of him. Dreams thus becomes a powerful medium for the transmission of satanic influences and powers. For proper understanding, we shall look at a few examples.

First, one may find himself being pursued by masquerades, human beings or dangerous animals such lions, bears and tigers. The intention is to kill the person targeted. If the attacker succeeds in knocking down his victim in the dream life, it would ultimately lead to real death in the physical world. The emergence of these strange beings who, or which, sometimes are known to the person being attacked, is an indication of imminent trouble to them. One major feature of such a dream is great perspiration at the time of waking up from one's sleep. On gaining his consciousness, the next thing a prospective victim does is to seek for a means of refuge by contacting the herbalist within his vicinity or look for any secret cult to shelter him from the impending doom. However, in the words of the writer of the book of Ecclesiastes, this is still 'vanity of vanity, all is vanity' (Eccl. 1:2). Such efforts will prove futile in the long run.

However, the case is different with a Christian, because he knows exactly what to do and where to run – he takes refuge 'in the name of the LORD [which] is a strong tower' (Prov. 18:10). The point needs to be made here that while there is a sure promise for Christians since, 'the sceptre of wickedness shall not rest...on the righteous' (Ps. 125:3), sometimes, the wicked may want to test their vaunted powers on the believers.[18] The consequences of such attempts are disastrous for satanic agents.

Secondly, regular sexual intercourse with the opposite sex in dreams is a major attack that can bring about the problem of impotence for a man or barrenness for a woman. There can be persistent sexual intercourse in dreams so much so that on wakening there would be real physical manifestation in form of deposit of semen. When this happens there can be no pregnancy. Even when a woman is pregnant, after such a dream abortion will naturally follow.

In the same way, if one is always receiving babies from strange beings in a dream, this is an indication of spiritual children. The essence of such dreams is to cause barrenness. One major feature of such an experience is immediate menstruation on waking up the following morning. This is a battle that is not physical. Appearance in the dream cannot be taken for reality. Even when the attacker in the dream happened to be a known person, it will be wrong to accuse such person in real life situation as being responsible for inflicting pains or childlessness. This is why such a battle is a spiritual one. You cannot rise up in the real physical world with the intention of fighting the person who has appeared to you in the dream arena. How will you substantiate your claim?

Attacks in dreams have no respect for sexuality or personalities. Males and females, Christians and non-Christians, alike fall victims. However, what makes the difference as noted above is that one group knows what to do for immediate cancellation of the operations of the powers and principalities, while the other group does not. The main objective of this attack is to make life miserable for the victims. Take, for instance, a man who gave a vivid explanation of his impotence:

> He was married for fifteen years, and used to dream that he was having sex with a heartthrob on a regular basis. To his amazement he could have sex better in his dream than in real life. After ten years of marriage, he eventually subjected himself to medical tests. It was discovered that he had low sperm count, but for five years there was no solution to his problem. Why the low sperm count? The answer is in the sexual enjoyment he was having with impersonating spirit being.[19]

A word of caution is appropriate here. This kind of experience may be pushed aside with a wave of the hand by anyone who is foreign to the experience of this man and be regarded as a nonsense or mere superstition. Yet the fact remains that deliverance from this manner of impotence cannot be achieved through a medical cure, but rather by placing one's faith in the Lord Jesus Christ. The man in question only found cure for his impotence after the gospel message was presented to him as the power of God for salvation. In his own words of testimony, he confirmed that having placed his trust in Christ, he became an overcomer, and his impotence was healed. Today, he is a happy father of boys and girls.

When witches and wizards appear to their victims in the spirit world (in their sleep or dream), they can shoot at them, pierce them with an arrow, or remove babies from the wombs of expectant women to cause miscarriage. They can even exchange normal children for demonic ones. Whatever they do in the spirit world has negative effects on their victims in the physical world.

A pertinent example of an attack that happened in the dream life of an individual, which manifested in a real life situation, was reported in the Vanguard Newspaper of Thursday, 21st June, 2001. It was an experience of a Commissioner in one of the States in Yorubaland. The Commissioner reported the mysterious death of his wife, Atinuke, because he had refused to be involved in an extra-marital relationship with a businesswoman. For refusing to have any relationship with her, the woman decided to target the wife, who was perceived as the stumbling block. In narrating his experience, the Commissioner recounts:

> I can't say precisely when Atinuke's illness began, but it started when she cried out in her sleep one night. I rushed into her room to find her rolling in pain. She announced that something had hit her like an arrow in the chest. She soon calmed down and we all went back to sleep. The next day, she couldn't get up from bed, insisting she was still feeling the pain, I advised her to go to the hospital. We were informed that she'd sustained a mild heart attack, had high blood pressure and should take things easy generally. She was placed on some drugs and we thought that was the end. But the pains did not subsidise, rather it grew worse. Sometimes, she would complain of stomach ache, then movement in her tummy, problem with breathing, headache, you name it. She lost her appetite and rapidly grew into a shadow of her old bubbly self. It got everyone worried, including friends and relations, and suggestion poured in from every corner. She was taken to several churches, Alfas, and eventually we degenerated into visiting traditional healers. It was in one of such places, somewhere in Osun State that the cat was let out of the bag. I was informed that my wife was being punished for debarring my association with a lover.[20]

Unfortunately, since their sinister acts are always carried out in the spirit world, their victims are under perpetual fear of bondage. They are not able to challenge them openly for the fear of being accused of wrong allegations. Yes, witches and wizards are the dreads of their society, and they exercise undue authority over their victims.

While their activities are mostly carried out in the dead of night,[21] they can also bring their wicked act to bear on the lives of innocent people in the daytime.[22] Witches and wizards are desperately wicked. Having inflicted spiritual and emotional wounds on their victims, they would also be the first to come and console and commiserate with them. The experience of this Commissioner also confirms this. Again he recounts:

> She [the business woman] paid me a visit in the office...to express her condolence. I brushed her off insisting that I'd seen the handwriting on the wall. But she denied it, indirectly warning that I should back off.[23]

Indeed the agents of darkness are merciless. They are always looking for ways to make life miserable for people. Even the so-called white witchcraft that claims to act for good purposes operates at the expense of innocent people to rob them of their joy and peace. Nothing is good in witchcraft. Those involved in it are 'spiritual hosts of wickedness in the heavenly places', working against the plan of God for the good of human beings created after His image.

The use of magic

The use of magic as a weapon of spiritual warfare among the Yoruba is significant. Magic, simply put, is the use of nature or supernatural forces for the singular aim of achieving one's most desired ends. In other words, magic is synonymous with using every available means at one's disposal to bring benefits to self. In this sense, it does not matter even if one needs to destroy the life of the other person being attacked insofar as there is a complete safeguarding of personal interests. Thus magic is an attempt to tap into and control the supernatural powers or resources of the universe for personal benefits.

Again, just like witchcraft, one can distinguish between 'good' and 'bad' magic. Good magic is expected to bring about good effects: to cure, to protect, and profit a person. Bad magic is meant to produce bad effects: to harm or hinder a person's progress. They can be referred to as white and black magic respectively. The use of magic to bring the desired result is not automatic. There are some taboos to be observed to make it functional, and when violated they can bring disastrous effects on the initiator. Also closely tied to the use of magic are *incantations*.

It is important to note at this juncture that while the children of light are not so wise in their own generation (Luke 16:8) as to know the truth of the Scripture that, 'Death and life are in the power of the tongue' (Prov. 18:21), those in the kingdom of darkness know this truth and exploit it to bring many into bondage. Satan was able to deceive Adam and Eve in the Garden of Eden by using deceptive words, a mere perversion of the word spoken by God (Gen. 3:1-3), simply because Adam and Eve had not 'kept the word of God in their heart' (Ps. 119:11). In trying to do the same with Jesus Christ he met with his failure. On this occasion, Christ used the power of the spoken word to destroy the cunning wiles of Satan by quickly affirming the truth of what has been written in the Bible (Luke 4:1-13).

Satan knows the power of the spoken word. Like Pharaoh's magicians who sought to duplicate the miracle of God in the turning of the rod to a serpent (Exod. 7:8-13), Satan would seek to adulterate whatever genuine power exits in the kingdom of God. No wonder, when Satan sends out his own word, it is 'to steal, to kill and destroy' (John 10:10). This is the backdrop against which we must see the use of incantations by Africans. For an African, the power of the spoken word is a major tool to make magic functional as a weapon of spiritual warfare. The above is not a digression, but simply to show the power of the spoken word as being used in the kingdom of darkness.

In magic the use of effigy is of paramount importance. It is employed to bring calamities on the victims in connexion with imitative magic. There are symbolic objects that are made to represent supernatural entities from which one expects some strange actions to issue out. For instance, a particular wood may be carved into the image of a divinity to be petitioned for a release of power from the spirit world to fight some targeted enemies. The wooden image to the person in question has a spirit in it, hence when he stands before it to make any request; it is with the belief that a message is being sent for the other person to be attacked. Again this is done in the context of incantations. Before the person being attacked knows what is happening, strange things would have happened which, if care is not taken, could result in his death.

In a similar manner, an effigy of a purported enemy could be made to represent his physical presence at the scene where the wicked act is to be performed. Such an effigy may be shot in the spirit world to command the death of the victim wherever he is. More than often, when the gun is fired, after series of incantations had preceded the shooting, the next news that is heard is the death of the attacked person. It is important to note that not every death in the course of sleeping was due to the problem of heart failure, as it is always claimed in the medical world. Most of the times, it could be the result of the operations carried out by the powers of darkness in the spirit world. This is an effective way of engaging in spiritual warfare among the Yoruba people. While the victim or relatives may not know the source of the attack, and or the cause of the death, the perpetrator knows what he had done. Hence he rejoices at the fulfillment of his wicked devices.

Again, when somebody is to be killed with a spiritual gun, a carved idol representing the image of the victim may be placed at the bottom of an *Iroko* tree. The spirit-man of the victim is then invoked, and after some words of incantations a gun is fired at the carved image. As the gun is fired, the victim simultaneously screams at home and dies.

In another way, the use of magic as a weapon of spiritual warfare can be from a contagious point of view. Contagious magic anticipates the desired result by merely establishing point of contact with any objects connected to the targeted enemy. This is different from the imitation method. If an individual wants to harm his victim he only needs to collect some ash from his hearth, a few sands from the ground on which he had urinated, a bit of his nail, or hairs from his head. By treating any of the objects collected from his victim magically, he believes whatever happens to these objects will, as a matter of certainty, happen to the victim. That is why people will not just throw away their nails after cutting them or allow their hairs to be thrown away, for fear of being taken hold of by their enemies.

It does not require the physical presence of the victim to take life out of him. By treating magically objects or materials he has once had contact with, he could be harmed physically wherever he is. In other words, distance is not a barrier to contagious magic. Awolalu and Dopamu have rightly observed this:

> A man can be harmed through his hair, nails, clothing, sleeping mat, placenta, navel cord, faeces, spittle, footprint, chewing stick, and anything that belongs to him. Even his name is regarded as belonging to him, and can be harmed through it. That is why people take care of anything, and everything that belongs to them to avoid an enemy getting hold of them for harmful intention. Parents bury the placenta and navel cord of their babies without allowing people to see them.[24]

Take for instance the case of Mr. White, who was perceived by Mr. Green to be a threat to him. Mr. Green saw Mr. White as a stumbling block because he did not allow him the free use of a section of the neighbourhood. In the opinion of Mr White, the construction of any drainage system would pose some danger to his building. The next thing that Mr. Green did was to treat the only passable route magically so that Mr. White could develop swollen feet that would culminate in his death. Truly, Mr. Green's diabolical act worked so much that by merely passing through that designated path, Mr. White was affected, and this resulted in his death in a matter of a few months. Though the magical power was not seen, yet it caught up with the victim and terminated his life abruptly.[25]

In other words, an attacker does not need personal physical contact to inflict misery on his victim. This is because the release of magic is by special powers acquired from demonic forces. Indeed, the consciousness of spiritual warfare has driven many people to be keenly attracted to magic as their weapons to fight both seen and unseen battles. It is always shocking to hear what people go through and suffer in the kingdom of darkness simply because they want protection. A member of my congregation once told me how deep he was in the practice of magic before his experience of new life in Christ. Specifically, there was a room in his house that neither his wife nor children could enter because of the deposits of charms to which some taboos had been attached. Any slightest violation of these taboos would result in serious consequences, not only for the affected person, but for him as well.

The use of charms
The use of charms is closely related to magic. Charms are of different forms. It could be a ring worn on one of the fingers. It could be a leather waistband. It could be other objects, which are of great significance to the initiator of the charms.[26] Charms are worn or kept in hidden places to avoid undue attention. A ring may be worn for the purpose of just patting the back of the victims or shaking the hands of the victims to transfer some misfortunes to them. In a sense, a victim does not know that an exchange of powers has taken place, or may not be aware that something negative has been done to him in the spiritual realm. Ignorance is no excuse. If care is not taken, this singular action of the transfer of power from the spirit world will affect him and alter his destiny for life.

Charm can equally be a representative object through which powers of darkness can operate. Take, for instance, the use of a clay doll, which is called among the Yoruba, *Sigidi*. Primarily this object operates to kill. Here again, incantations play significant role. This clay doll is sent with words of incantations to go and visit the house of the victim. It goes with a whip or rod in its hand to injure the victim by killing him. The appearance of this strange object creates great fear in the victim as it walks terrifyingly towards him. What it does is to strike the victim. Having struck the victim in the spirit world, instant death is expected in the physical world; and often such is the inevitable result.

This clay doll cannot be seen physically by anyone except by the person being attacked. Yet the result of the operation is a deadly one. It is important to note that this clay doll has no power of its own except the demonic powers manifesting themselves through it. Indeed, it is a dangerous thing not to be in Christ where there is sure protection on a moment-by-moment basis. But for those in Christ, 'He [God] frustrates the devices of the crafty, so that their hands cannot carry out their [wicked] plans' (Job 5:12).

Enlistment in the membership of secret cults
The quest for safety for an African does not stop until he has practically satisfied himself that he has got the best form of protection through personal efforts. Thus he goes from one level to another to acquire more superior demonic powers. In this regard, enlistment in secret cults is regarded as one of the highest levels to which one can aspire in order to be vested with *sure powers*. With the idea that the whole life is full of battles, people enlist in secret cults for three specific reasons.

The first reason is for defensive purpose. That is to say, people seek to get involved in cultism to be sure of their safety in the face of the many dangers of life. Coupled with this is the desire to prosper and become recognized in the society.

Secondly, people join secret cults in order to take revenge on their enemies. Probably due to some personal imagination, an individual may think that the enemy has caused the misfortune around him, and he may wish to retaliate. The effective way to do this is to enlist in a secret cult that would promise to fight injustice for its members.

Thirdly, people join secret cults solely for the purpose of perpetrating evil. There are people who are just satanic in their manner of life. All that they think is how to make life miserable for other people. This group of people, despite committing great atrocities, can still seek for refuge in secret cults. There is no doubt that secret cults in their manner of operation are effective weapons in the kingdom of darkness.

By definition, a cult is the coming together of a number of people with the same motif bound together by an oath of secrecy, usually a blood covenant, to make the oath so taken irrevocable. By virtue of this oath, a member is under obligation to support another member at all times irrespective of the situations that demand such support. This explains largely why many people take refuge in these cults. People are lured into cults simply because they want power, protection and wealth, without bothering whether the acquisition of such wealth places them in direct opposition to God. It is not our aim to go into how people get enlisted in these cults. We shall be satisfied here only with how they carry out their sinister activities.

Secret cults are of various degrees. The common ones are: The Reformed *Ogboni* Fraternity, *Ogboni Ibile*, and the Lodge. Though some of these cults pretend to be highly religious, and may even involve the name of Jesus Christ in their practices,[27] or threaten court action for calling them secret societies, yet the fact still remains that they are not to be mistaken as people who walk in the light. Testimonies of those who were once members, but were rescued by the power of Christ, confirm the esoteric nature of these cults. They are deadly in their operations and keep their members in bondage of death in case of any breach of the oath of secrecy which they entered into at the time of their initiation. The initiation rites mark the starting point of admission into their membership, and this is always a dreadful experience. According to evangelist Joshua Balogun, initiation into the Reformed *Ogboni* Fraternity often takes place in the vestry of a church building, in which a clergyman would lead the ceremony.[28] Though they may claim to be harmless, and pretend that they are just social group for the purpose of fellowship, that is far from being the case since what goes on among them leaves much to be desired.

Secret cults operate by principle of association. In other words, if any member is offended, the whole group is offended. Their mode of operation is quite similar to the operations of witchcraft. They rely on the use of magic, charms and incantations to deal ruthlessly with their victims. They afflict from the spiritual realm. To them there is no forgiveness for any offender. The ultimate aim is to destroy and bring misery upon their victims.[29]

Though our intention here is not to pre-empt our discussion in the next chapter, yet it is essential to know what the mind of God is concerning these weapons of spiritual warfare at the disposal of the Africans. In other words, what does the Scripture say about these African weapons of spiritual warfare? The Bible does not mince words about the displeasure of God for employing any of these 'so called' *powers*. God frowns at occultism. The penalty for engaging in sorcery, witchcraft, magic, medium and use of charms is death (Exod. 22:18; Lev. 20:6; Deut. 18:10-13). No wonder, the more people seek for salvation in these powers, the more they bring untold hardship upon themselves. This is simply because these are powerless powers when put side by side with the power of God. Acquisition of any of these powers for the purpose of security is tantamount to going into the bondage of Satan.

Conclusion

To conclude the discussion in this chapter, let me give a brief summary of the major points. First, our focus has been on the reality of spiritual warfare among the Yoruba, looking at the various battles of life that must be fought in order to keep above its vicissitudes. Secondly, we noted that it does not matter whether you have offended anybody or not – your success in life is enough to make you an object of attack. Thirdly, the reasons for which people seek refuge from the kingdom of darkness is to find security. This they do by attempting to acquire various powers to equip themselves against the innumerable battles of life, whether through the practice of witchcraft, the use of magic, the acquisition of charms, and enlistment in the membership of secret cults.

However, while people seek for refuge and protection from these different sources, unfortunately the reverse is the case. Rather than finding protection, they are lured into greater bondage. The anguish and frustration in the lives of multitudes that have taken refuge in these satanic ways bear witness to the truth of the gospel that there is no salvation in any other name, apart from the name of Jesus. He is the only power that can give sure protection. This is the subject to be discussed in the next two chapters.

7

Powers In Encounter With Power:
(1) Christ the Deliverer

Introduction

What makes the gospel so powerful that is able to dislodge Satan from his stronghold in the lives of many Africans? What is unique in the gospel message that accounts for its conquest of the powers and principalities so that people willingly surrendered their lives to Christ? The answer is quite simple. Those under the oppressive rule of demonic powers mainly turn to the gospel message in attempt to find sure release from distress. Those in distress believe that such a release would end the taunting powers of the dark kingdom in their lives. In turn this release will bring in a reign of peace and assurance of a more fulfilled life.

As we commence our discussion here our main objective is to see demonic forces as real powers, who regularly put up a strong fight to keep their victims in perpetual custody. In other words, they do not merely exercise demonic influence, but they are 'power designates' seeking to frustrate humankind. As Schlier writes:

> They do not merely possess power and the other attributes, they are power. They are not just something or somebody, and also have power. They exist as power, etc. That is what they are called, and they get these names because that is how they manifest themselves and their being. And that is why...St. Paul enumerates them in the same breath with such phenomena as life, present, future, height, and depth. Evidently while they are powers of existence, dominating, embracing, determining powers, they have something in common with these other enumerated phenomena. That common element is their nature as power, as threatening superior power [1]

It is not surprising therefore that the victims of the powers and principalities are powerless, and are in total bondage to them because they exercise over their victims a form of authority that they have no right to challenge. In the light of the above, it is quite obvious that only a stronger power could rescue humanity from demonic forces as *power designate.*

Herein lies the preaching of the gospel as the revelation of the 'power of God for salvation' (Rom. 1:16), to rescue humanity from the *powers of darkness.* In proclaiming the gospel, the *power of God* is presented as a direct response to destroy the *powers of darkness.* As the message of the gospel is presented as the power of God, it means different experiences for various people at their points of need. As Warneck writes:

> The gospel contains many diverse powers...the diversity of its gifts renders it acceptable to diverse people. To the Jew it commends itself as the religion of fulfilled prophecy; to the Greek as the true wisdom; to the Roman as the perfect law; to the German as the ideal service of the Lord.[2]

Thus, the preaching of the gospel means *power* to various people depending on their needs for divine intervention. Jesus Christ as the 'power of God for salvation' can be seen from different angles. To those whose life of abject poverty was changed by accepting Christ, He is the power to make wealth (Deut. 8:18, cf. Phil. 4:19). To those who trusted in Christ and they were saved from their hopeless situation, Christ is the power for hope (Rom. 15:13). To the preachers of the gospel who go about casting out demons and healing people, Christ is the power for signs and wonders (Mark 16:16ff.).

Jesus Christ, who is the power and wisdom of God, is also our righteousness (Jer. 23:6), healer (Isa. 53:5), redeemer (Isa. 59:20), peace (Eph. 2:14), and hope (Col. 1:27). It follows then that any of these attributes of Christ, when exemplified in the preaching of the gospel, is capable of demonstrating the power of God to bring victory over the operations of the principalities and powers. What a person under the oppressive rule of Satan wants is the message that is able to set him free from the enslaving powers of the kingdom of darkness and which at the same time is able to guarantee sustained victory in the days ahead. As long as there is a manifestation of such power, the message will be readily embraced. Herein lies the sufficiency of the message of the gospel as power of God for salvation for Africans who are fighting both seen and unseen battles.

The gospel as the proclamation of the power of God

The kingdom of Satan is built upon lies. The preaching of the gospel message is the proclamation of the power of God at work to set the captives free from the lies of the devil. The Scripture bears witness to this truth, 'Therefore if the Son makes you free, you shall be free indeed' (John 8:36). Always, the devil seeks to threaten people from being saved as he moves them to deny the truth of the message of the gospel. What he does is to create fear in the hearts of those being saved that they will die, and or that some other catastrophes will befall them should they attempt to quit the kingdom of darkness. However, they will not die, but live. This is because, having been saved by Christ, they have passed from death to life (1 John 3:14). Take for instance the personal testimony of Emmanuel Eni, in his book titled, *Delivered from the Power of Darkness*:

On the 1st of May 1985, a month after my conversion, at about 2.00 a.m. while others in the house were asleep, I was awakened by these agents [of the Queen of the coast]. They commanded me to walk out of the house. I obeyed, walked out and they followed behind. We moved on to the burial ground by St. Paul's Anglican Church, off Aba Road, Port Harcourt. On reaching there they said, 'You must come back. If you refuse we will kill you or make you destitute.' After this instruction they left. I regained my senses and wondered how I came into the burial ground at that time of the night. I walked back home; my late uncle's wife asked me where I went. I never answered her, rather I went back to bed and slept. They decided to attack me in the afternoons. At times, while walking along the road they would fight me. Others around would see me fighting with the air or see me running as if being pursued. I alone would be seeing them.[3]

To a man deeply involved in cultism and under regular demonic attack, the gospel is worthy of acceptance simply because it is the

good news which meets the urgent need of his life for salvation
(Ps. 91:1-2). In the light of the message of the gospel that brings
about instant transformation in his life, he becomes conscious of
his helplessness, folly and unprofitable past drenched in satanic
activities.

The preaching of the gospel comes with a definite agenda to
announce a message of liberation from the shackles of the enemy
to those engrossed in the world of misery. Perhaps, this is the reason
why Satan is always opposed to the preachers of the gospel, and
will do everything possible to ensure that man does not profit by
the word. 'The sower sows the word.... And when they hear, Satan
comes immediately and takes away the word that was sown in
their heart' (Mark 4:15). There is always an open confrontation to
challenge the authority of the preacher in order to detract him from
preaching the word. 'Now there was a man in their synagogue
with an unclean spirit. And he cried out, saying, 'Let us alone!
What have we to do with You, Jesus of Nazareth? Did You come
to destroy us'' (Mark 1:23-24)?

Indeed, there are those operating in the kingdom of darkness
who are completely ignorant of the power of the gospel. When the
messenger of the good news comes, their reaction will be very
similar to what the Athenians said of Paul, 'What does this babbler
want to say?' (Acts 17:18). Fully saturated with the powers of
darkness, they believe there is nothing such a preacher will say
that can nullify or cancel the potency of their satanic powers. Such
people will wilfully come to crusades or revival meetings as
emissaries from the kingdom of darkness to oppose the preacher
of the gospel. But before they knew what was happening, the power
from on high will have caught up with them, rendered them
powerless, and consequently brought them on their knees in
obedience to the Lordship of Christ.

A pertinent example in this direction was the example of Sade
Fadipe. In her personal testimony after her conversion experience,
she narrated how she had been sent from the kingdom of darkness
to go and disrupt the revival being conducted at Ogbomoso by
evangelist Kayode Williams:

In 1987 there was a seven-day big crusade organised in Ogbomoso where evangelist Kayode Williams was to preach. It was to be an evangelistic crusade that would cause a great depopulation in the kingdom of darkness. This was a great upset for us in the kingdom of darkness. In order to make this crusade impossible, I volunteered to go and cause a problem for the organisers of this crusade. The method I adopted was to go and cause rain to fall so as to disrupt the crusade. For three days I had caused rain to fall, disrupting the programme, and almost paralysed the efforts of the organisers of the crusade. However, in spite of the heavy downpour of rain, the crusade had continued uninterrupted. This was a great problem for us in the kingdom of darkness, and we decided to change the method of operation by deciding to imprison the spirit man of the evangelist in a *tin of milo*. The intention was to shoot the spirit man of the evangelist with a gun in the spirit world, causing his instant death and thus ending abruptly the crusade. On the fourth day, by the word of knowledge, the evangelist knew that the rain that fell in the past three days was the handiwork of the agents of Satan. Hence on the fourth day as the crusade was about to begin, the evangelist prayed and took authority over the prince of the air, principalities and powers. Specifically, he challenged the powers of darkness that night that if they tried to cause rain to fall, whoever the agents, he would command the ground to open and swallow them. At that point, my whole body was set on fire, and so I could no longer stand on the crusade ground. That was how I left and went back to report in the kingdom of darkness that I could not stand the power of the man of God when he started to pray. That was how no rain fell that night, and the crusade continued uninterrupted.[4]

Indeed, the power of the gospel message is the power of authority, which when brought in face-to-face encounter with the operations of the powers and principalities they are made to tremble. The author of the book of Acts writes:

> Now when they had gone through the island to Paphos, they found a certain sorcerer, a false prophet, a Jew whose name was Bar-Jesus, who was with the proconsul, Sergius Paulus, an intelligent man. This man called for Barnabas and Saul and sought to hear the word of God. But Elymas the sorcerer…withstood them, seeking to turn the proconsul away from the faith. Then Saul, who is also called Paul, filled with the Holy Spirit, looked intently at him and said, 'O full of

all deceit and all fraud, you son of the devil, you enemy of all righteousness, will you not cease perverting the straight ways of the Lord. And now, indeed, the hand of the Lord is upon you, and you shall be blind, not seeing the sun for a time.' And immediately a dark mist fell on him, and he went around seeking someone to lead him by the hand (Acts 13:6-11).

The uncertainty of the future is what drives an unbeliever to seek help and guidance from the kingdom of darkness. In the operations of the powers and principalities, an unbeliever depends on demonic spirits to bring *words of assurance* to him that he is safe in the face of the vicissitudes of life. No wonder, when such words are brought, they are obeyed simply because they are portrayed as messages capable of bringing deliverance.[5] This, regrettably, has been the driving force behind unbelievers' quest to seek protection from many cults as mentioned in chapter 6. Again, such is the background of the people the preacher of the gospel comes across in the process of proclaiming the good news of salvation from the kingdom of darkness. The only condition that can convince unbelievers of the futility of their so-called *powers* is seeing the power of the gospel demolishing the forces of darkness on which they depended.

Herein comes the need for great assurance on the part of the preacher of the gospel who is preaching the message of salvation to those entangled in the web of Satan. He must be sure of the power working in him and through him. He must be able to bring the message to his audience with great conviction like Peter and John who said, 'Silver and gold I do not have, but what I have I give you: In the name of Jesus Christ of Nazareth, rise up and walk' (Acts 3:6). He must be confident to declare like Paul, 'For I am not ashamed of the gospel of Christ, for it is the power of God to salvation for everyone who believes' (Rom. 1:16).

The point is that the messenger of the good news must be fully aware that Satan is not happy that his kingdom is being exploited. Therefore, it is a matter of a strong and fierce battle. Jesus Christ Himself underscores the fierceness of this battle, when He said to His disciples, 'And from the days of John the Baptist until now the kingdom of heaven suffers violence, and the violent take it by force' (Matt. 11:12). The preacher of the good news must first come fully armed in the power of the Holy Spirit, to be able to bring the message of liberation to those in the captivity of the powers of darkness.

The purpose for which the preacher comes with the gospel is to remove any doubts from those in the 'den of lions' that Christ is the only solution to their problems and that he has the power to deliver them from all the powers of darkness. As Warneck writes:

> If the messenger of the Gospel, therefore, wishes to make any impression, he must himself have sure convictions. Should he come without the assurance that he is bringing them the absolute and true religion, his words will find no echo in the hearts hungering for certainty.[6]

He must be sure of what he is presenting to them so much so that if it means dying for it, he must be ready. In other words, he must be sure of the power of the message to be able to say like Paul, 'What do you mean by weeping and breaking my heart? For I am ready, not only to be bound, but also to die at Jerusalem for the name of the Lord Jesus' (Acts 21:13). When preaching the good news to those in bondage to demonic powers, it must be realised that Satan is attacking aggressively from his kingdom. In the light of this, the preacher must be fully armed, sure of the power at his disposal and be ready to declare the exclusive power of the gospel: 'Nor is there salvation in any other, for there is no other name under heaven given among men by which we must be saved' (Acts 4:12).

What Satan hates is the confession of the saved soul as he bears witness to the deliverance the Lord has wrought in his life as he proclaims the good news of his salvation. Satan will attempt to deprive the believer from using the effective weapon of testifying to the power of the gospel, knowing for sure that others who hear the words of his testimony will equally overcome him 'by the blood of the Lamb and the word of their testimony' (Rev. 12:11).

This verse of this Scripture is very significant for our task here. The preacher of the good news must be aware of the power in the blood of Jesus. He must sound out the good news that as many as have trusted Christ have become untouchable for the powers of darkness. Preachers of the good news must proclaim with confidence that when Jesus Christ shed His blood on the cross at Calvary, it became the great witness to Satan and his rebellious cohorts (the powers and principalities) that they have lost the battle.

The blood of the Lamb of God that takes away the sins of the world is the blood that marks out Christians for security: 'For indeed Christ, our Passover, was sacrificed for us' (1 Cor. 5:7). Just as the blood of the lamb sacrificed at the Passover became the sure sign of protection for the Israelites at the eve of their departure from the land of Egypt (Exod. 12:13), so in a greater dimension the blood of Christ becomes the eternal mark of deliverance and security for as many as have trusted in His atoning work on the cross at Calvary

This blood has purchased the believer (1 Cor. 6:20 cf. 1 Pet. 1:18-19) and has marked him out as God's property too dangerous for Satan to tamper with. Yes, when in the face of danger, if the believer remembers to plead the power in this blood, there is sure victory for him over Satan. No wonder the writer of 1 John mentions the uniqueness of this blood, as he writes, 'For there are three that bear witness in heaven: the Father, the Word, and the Holy Spirit; and these three are one. And there are three that bear witness on earth: the Spirit, the water, and the blood; and these three agree as one' (1 John 5:7-8). If the voice of Abel's blood cries from the ground against Cain for the justification of Abel before God (Gen. 4:10), much more shall the blood of Jesus Christ the Mediator of a new covenant 'speaks better things than the blood of Abel' (Heb. 12:24).

Believers must be encouraged to know that by pleading the blood of Jesus there is immediate covering for them in face of harassment from the kingdom of darkness. By appealing to the power in this blood, he is immediately seated above the principalities and powers, above dominion and might (Eph. 1:21). The mentioning of the blood by the believer is a witness against the serpent of old; that the 'Seed of the woman' has completely bruised his head. This is the sense in which the author of the book of Revelation writes, 'And they overcame him by the blood of the

Lamb' (Rev. 12:11). No matter the nature of the war that Satan and his emissaries put up against a child of God, on pleading the blood, the foes are vanquished.

Thus in the preaching of the good news, Christ must be presented as the redeemer and Saviour who has 'destroyed him who has the power of death, that is, the devil' (Heb. 2:14). The specific way he did this was through his death. Since Christ is alive, and His blood speaks better things on our behalf, we can plead the same for our safety. David Peterson rightly notes this as he writes, 'The blood of Christ is the most powerful of all,'[7] because His blood is the payment that sets us free from the punishment for our sin, and therefore all the accusations of Satan cannot hold against believers. Writing further, Peterson maintains, 'We have continuing right of access to "the sanctuary" of God's presence "by the blood of Jesus" and because of his ongoing priestly rule "over the house of God" (Heb. 10:19-21).'[8] In other words, the shedding of this blood at Calvary guarantees the eternal security of believers as long as they remain in covenant relationship with God. This is the sense in which for believers, 'He who sits in the secret place of the Most High shall abide under the shadow of His Almighty' (Ps. 91:1). This is the truth that Satan will vehemently oppose from becoming real to those who are listening to the gospel message.

What Satan does is to encourage non-Christians to discountenance the message of salvation and believe instead in magicians or soothsayers. Even though they might have been deceived many times, he makes them to trust the empty promises of the magicians and magical acts to which they were previously exposed. The reasons for which he does this is that he does not want them to know anything about the truth that can set them free. The entire system of the kingdom of darkness is built on lies. Satan will suggest to his victims that he is able to offer them security in the face of many uncertainties of life, whereas he is actually bringing them into a greater bondage of fear.

He will suggest to them that he has the gift of life, whereas what he is offering them in a subtle manner is the gift of death. Thus from the moment unbelievers are caught up in his web they are left to live in the fear of death until the liberating power of the gospel comes in to deliver them. When the gospel comes to those in bondage to the demonic spirits, their minds previously darkened and brutalised by the fear of satanic worship are liberated. For them, there is full appreciation of the power of the gospel to save. In the light of the encounter which they already had with the liberating power of the gospel they can declare like the blind man healed of his blindness from birth, 'That though I was blind, now I see' (John 9:25).

Bringing the message of the gospel to those under demonic attack and oppression is to assure them that we are presenting them with a power stronger than the one to which they have been enslaved. In other words, the gospel of Jesus is the power that unbelievers[9] need to give them security and peace amid the uncertainties of life. When they accept the free offer of salvation given by Christ, they instantaneous 'pass over from death to life' (1 John 3:14).

Deliverance as salvation from the bondage of fear

Since the practice of magic or enlistment in the membership of cultic institutions is the brainchild of the powers and principalities, Christians must seek sharper weapons for their defence as they preach the good news.[10] Hence Paul writes, 'For though we walk in the flesh, we do not war according to the flesh. For the weapons of our warfare are not carnal, but mighty through God for pulling down of strongholds, casting down argument and every high thing that exalts itself against the knowledge of God, bringing every thought into captivity to the obedience of Christ' (2 Cor. 10:3-5).

The demons have powers. Such powers put together are hurtful and injurious to humans. Often in critical and life-threatening situations, people come to appreciate the power of God to deliver. At such times, they see the stark reality of the impotence of their charms, the uselessness of the plethora of their regular sacrifices, and the futility of capitalising on their membership of cultic institutions. The mighty move of the power of God to deliver at such critical times is the best testimony to the incomparable power of the gospel!

Unbelievers are bound by the fears of the powers and principalities. But through the preaching of the good news the weaponries of the kingdom of darkness are destroyed in the name of Jesus, the conqueror of sin and the devil. When people are brought forth, and prayed for with healing and deliverance following, nothing can change them from following the Lord Jesus Christ in whose name such miracles were wrought. As we have noted in the last chapter, what many unbelievers have to wrestle with primarily is not the problem of how to conquer sin in their lives. Rather, their main preoccupation is how to escape from the kingdom of darkness in which they are tightly bound. This bondage is very overwhelming. It is reflected in the fears that surround them, be it fear of spirits or fear of human enemies seeking to inflict catastrophes either on the family, business, health or otherwise. These are the circumstances that have held many people spellbound to the powers and principalities for reasons of security. The experience of the inhabitants of a small town, Erinmo-Ijesa in Osun State, Nigeria as reported in *This Day Newspaper* of Thursday, April 5, 2001 is a ready example in this direction:

About 36 years ago, an intrepid young man challenged the local deity of a rustic western community to a fight. Unlike now, those were times when you could count on your fingers the numbers of Christians in a particular locality. Then, also, the scanty number of converts to the Christian faith still practised some sort of syncretism. Those who were genuine Christians were even fewer, just as the churches were few and far between. So it was almost a suicidal venture for anyone in the largely non-Christian community to not only undermine one of its idols but also desecrate it. Popularly worshipped by the handful of natives in Erinmo-Ijesa in Osun State, *Agindanyi*, the local god, was feared and revered by all the villagers except, as it is now seems obvious, Samuel Kayode Abiara, who was then 23. Not that he was innately irreligious, but because he hated with a passion anything that has to do with idol worship. Besides, he loved and trained to serve God from a very early age. Fired with such apostolic zeal, therefore, he led some members of his yet-to-be popular church to the shrine where the deity was worshipped and burnt it down. The action, he later said, was inspired by an instruction from God. Naturally, the village folk, the majority of them idol worshippers, pronounced a curse on the daring chap. For his sacrilegious act, they declared, death would come knocking at his door in seven days time. He survived the ominous oral missile deployed to snuff out his life. And, as if to rub salt on injury, a mighty church which he oversees now occupies the same spot where the shrine once stood. For the thousands of faithful of the Christ Evangelical Ministry International of Christ Apostolic Church, Agbala Itura, that was a significant litmus test for Prophet Abiara, the Church's founder and director general. It was to them, as with the example of Prophet Elijah pitted against the prophets of Baal, winning souls for God....and sustaining the faith of Christian worshippers in Nigeria and elsewhere.[11]

The good news is that the power of the gospel has come to loose people from the bondage of fear. Though the deliverance of people who have newly experienced the liberating power of the gospel was not a matter of acceptance of a Saviour who has redeemed them from the curse and power of sin, yet there is no doubt that the fact of their freedom without any personal efforts is the arrival of a more powerful God who has rescued them from the powers of darkness who had held sway over their lives for so long. While for them their deliverance was not much of a sin issue, yet insofar as they never went back to worship and pay homage to the forces of darkness in the garb of witchcraft, sorcery or ancestral gods, it was a deliverance from sin. This is simply because the worship of any other gods apart from the living God is sinful (Exod. 20:3).

It is important to know that to achieve true freedom from bondage to the power of Satan, there must be an entrance of the living power. A particular power brought about bondage, and it requires a stronger power to set free: 'When a strong man, fully armed, guards his own palace, his goods are in peace. But when a stronger than he comes upon him and overcomes him, he takes from him all his armour in which he trusted, and divides his spoils' (Luke 11:21-22).

In other words, God through His Son Jesus Christ, the deliverer of the enslaved humanity, has intervened divinely in the human situation to grant deliverance from the captivity of the powers of darkness. This freedom is brought about when the Word of God is preached. In the preaching of the Word, salvation from the power of darkness is rooted in the centrality of the cross. Hence Paul writes to the Corinthians, 'For the message of the cross is foolishness to those who are perishing, but to us who are being saved it is the power of God' (1 Cor. 1:18). Commenting on the centrality of the cross of Christ to the victory of Christians, Archbishop George Carey writes:

> Another way of looking at what the Cross means is by reminding ourselves of that language of Paul, about sin being a tyrant over us. Clearly, if we are at the mercy of tyrant, we need a *champion*, someone who will fight for us and set us free. So one picture way of understanding what Jesus did on the Cross is that of a champion or soldier who takes over our battle and defeats the dictator, finally leading him out chained and captive.[12]

In the preaching of the gospel an unbeliever in a childlike faith trusts Christ for what He has done and accepts the verdict of the good news for his present circumstance. When the power of the Deliverer comes in encounter with the powers from the kingdom of darkness, they must bow. Thus in the life of the person in bondage to satanic powers, there is immediate rescue operation from fear and dominion of demonic spirits. A new kingdom with a superior power has arrived and come to stay in the power of the Holy Spirit.

In a way that the individual who has just experienced the power of God in his life has never known before, there is an instant transformation from fear to peace. 'You will keep in perfect peace whose mind is stayed on You because he trust in You' (Isa. 26:3). There is a supernaturally initiated movement from the kingdom of darkness to the kingdom of light. There is divinely motivated crossing from death to life. The person who has just been liberated knows that 'all things have become new' (2 Cor. 5:17). Henceforth, he knows that he has not received 'the spirit of bondage again to fear, but [has] received the Spirit of adoption [into the kingdom of God]' (Rom. 8:15).

Anyone who has previously been in bondage to the powers of darkness will understand the mighty influence which the power of the gospel exerts. The testimony of those delivered from the kingdom of darkness cannot but make it attractive to those who are still under demonic influences. When one is in bondage to the powers of darkness, his actions are not his. He acts under an irresistible constraint. That is why it is possible for witches, wizards and those in cultic societies to kill their own blood relations with impunity, without any sense of guilt or shame.

Indeed, those in bondage to the powers of darkness are in total subjection to the powers and principalities. This is the sense in which those who have been freed by the power of Jesus from the captivity of Satan see Him as the self-revelation of God, the *Almighty*, the conqueror of demons and all satanic works. Their personal understanding of the power of the gospel makes it clear to them that indeed Christ has come to destroy the works of the devil (1 John 3:8). The result that the preaching of the gospel produces among the unbelievers after their conversion shows clearly that in the heart of the Christian faith is the reality of true redemption. The rescue operation that Christ carried out for those previously in bondage to demonic powers clearly demonstrates that indeed Christ has come to preach deliverance to those in bondage, to break the yoke of the strong man and set the captives free from oppression and pain of the kingdom of darkness.[13]

In turning to the gospel unbelievers desire to be delivered from the fear of evil spirits who are the bane of their life. Fear torments, and whatever torments is of the devil. For those of them who have experienced the power of the gospel, the power of Jesus Christ is greater than the power of ancestral spirits. Being in Christ now, there is nothing to fear any longer. When unbelievers are completely set free by the power of God, as Warneck has rightly noted:

> They no longer need to give up their cattle for sacrifices and festival; they are no longer compelled to involve themselves in debt to meet the demands of the priest; they are no longer afraid of the magicians and magic.[14]

Let all the forces of darkness gather together in their nocturnal meetings, the power of Christ will scatter them. The so-called powers will just be like an ordinary thread when it comes in contact with a burning fire. Indeed Christians can certainly declare that when the *powers of darkness* (the powers and principalities) come in face-to-face encounter with the *Power of God*, who is Christ, the powers of the magician will bow down, the powers of the cults will bow down, the powers behind the use of charms and amulets will bow down. Their song of victory will be, 'And who will harm *us* if *we* become followers of what is good?' (1 Pet. 3:13). Again, with all confidence they can affirm, 'He who is in *us* is greater than he who is in the world' (1 John 4:4). For the Africans who were once bound by the powers of darkness, it is the reality of the new life in Christ, as people who have already taken refuge in the 'strong tower' (Prov. 18:10), that assures them of the impotence of the powers and principalities.

The power of the gospel is what sets believers up for persecution by their former associates. Battles are constantly going on in the kingdom of darkness seeking to draw back those who have been delivered from bondage of the dark kingdom. However, no matter how hot the battles are, Christians remain secure, except when they voluntarily build a connecting bridge to their former manner of life. Those who were formerly revelling in satanic activities, driven about by forces of darkness beyond their control, are now enlisted in the Lord's army and are completely liberated from their tormentors as long as they hold on to the Word of God. It should be noted that only those who were once terribly bound to the spirit of fear could experience the great joy of being set free by the Son of God (John 8:36).

The result of the dramatic encounter of unbelievers with the Lord is the throwing away of their amulets and all the paraphernalia of cultic institutions (whether concealed or displayed in strategic places). The bringing forth of these weapons of the dark kingdom is with much confidence that saved souls no longer have any association with Satan (2 Cor. 6:14-16). Often this act is done in the presence of ministers of God who are there to strengthen the faith of the newly converted. After bringing out these weapons of darkness, they are set on fire, and the burning of them into ashes depicts the emptiness of the powers of Satan. This is a demonstration of the saved person's readiness to bind himself to Christ who has delivered him from the power of darkness. Thus in the words of Paul, they have 'turned to God from idols to serve the living and true God' (1 Thess. 1:9). This is the beginning of a new life in Christ. As he continues in this new life, there is the need for him to be on guard regularly so that Satan does not take advantage of him. He needs to be aware of the weapons at his disposal to keep Satan at bay. This is the subject to be addressed in the next chapter.

8

Powers in Encounter With Power: (2) Believers' Weapons of Spiritual Warfare

Although there is 'no condemnation for those who are in Christ Jesus' (Rom. 8:1), Satan still is regularly looking for ways to accuse believers before God. The focus of this chapter, therefore, is twofold. First, there is the need for believers to know that there is spiritual warfare ahead after they have been rescued from the kingdom of darkness, and secondly to inform them of the weapons at their disposal. Satan does not relinquish his office without a struggle. While it is true that each new convert has gained freedom from the strongholds of Satan, he still seeks to cause a derailment in their new life. Herein lies the importance of Paul's injunction to the church in Ephesus:

> Finally, my brethren, be strong in the Lord and in the power of His might. Put on the whole armour of God, that you may be able to stand against the wiles of the devil. For we do not wrestle against flesh and blood, but against principalities, against powers, against the rulers of the darkness of this age, against spiritual hosts of wickedness in the heavenly places (Eph. 6:10-12).

While Christians rejoice in the fact that, in the events of the death and resurrection of Christ, the critical battle has already been won, yet there is a sense in which the battle is still ongoing. Each Christian must continue to wrestle as he continues the Christian race. Hence in the words of O'Brien:

> The paragraph is neither 'an irrelevant appendix' to Ephesians nor 'a parenthetical aside' within it but a crucial element to which the rest of the epistle has been pointing. The 'full armour of God' which the readers are urged to put on as they engage in a deadly spiritual warfare (v. 11) is Yahweh's own armour, which he and his Messiah have worn and which is now provided for his people as they engage in battle.[1]

Though the above injunction is for believers, it is particularly relevant to a new Christian in order to maintain his balance in the faith. As noted earlier, what sometimes leads to an unbeliever's acceptance of Christ is not so much the consciousness of sin but the fear of the unknown powers. Insofar as he has been delivered, the need should be stressed that the worst thing that can happen is to venture back to his former way of life. Paul does not want believers to be ignorant of the devices of the devil. Thus, in the words of John Stott, the purpose of Ephesians 6:10-20, is:

> To warn us of their [the principalities and powers] hostility and teach us how to overcome them. Is it God's plan to create a new society? Then they will do their utmost to destroy it. Has God through Jesus Christ broken down the walls dividing human beings of different races and culture from each other? Then the devil through his emissaries will strive to rebuild them. Does God intend his reconciled and redeemed people to live together in harmony and purity? Then the powers of hell will scatter among them the seeds of discord and sin. It is with these powers that we are told to wage war, or – to be more precise – to 'wrestle.'[2]

Satan will put up a strong fight, so every believer faces a serious battle with the forces of darkness. But this battle is not a physical one; rather it is spiritual, and spiritual weapons will be required to fight it.

Paul begins his admonition to the Ephesians by encouraging them to 'be strong in the Lord and in the power of His might'. This is an imperative, a command to make conscious efforts to keep one's new standing in the Lord, who has made the new way of escape from the kingdom of darkness possible. In other words, a believer is expected to work out his 'salvation with fear and trembling', to use Paul's words in Philippians 2:12.

The use of the word 'Lord' has a significant implication for understanding 'the power of His might'. Elsewhere the title 'Lord' is synonymous with 'Christ' (Acts 16:31; Rom. 10:13), but here it is better understood as referring to God, who has anointed Christ 'with the Holy Spirit and power, who went about doing good and healing all who were oppressed by the devil' (Acts 10:38). This is the way Christ becomes the 'power of His might'. The word 'might' could also be understood as 'strength'. Therefore, Paul's reference to the 'power of His might' will be another way of saying, 'Christ, the power of God' (1 Cor. 1:24). Hence to be strong in Christ, who is the power of His might, is to be strong in God, into whose dominion the believer has been rescued. As a Jew, it would not be strange to Paul to understand the Lord God as a warrior. For example, Psalm 18:39 says: 'For you have armed me with strength for the battle; You have subdued under me those who rose up against me.' Verses such as this must have informed his injunction to believers in Ephesus to stand in Him who has the power to defend in His strength.

Having admonished the Ephesians to 'be strong in the Lord and in the power of His might', Paul continues with another imperative: 'Put on the whole armour of God' (6:11), the purpose being that believers 'be able to stand against the wiles of the devil'. Paul knows that only the 'whole armour' is sufficient to combat the wiles of Satan. For a soldier going to war, the whole armour was a requirement. Here again we see Christ as the 'whole armour of God', the whole power of God needed to combat the wiles of the devil.

What does it mean for a believer to put on Christ? To put on Christ is to be incorporated into His standing before God.[3] In other words, when a believer 'is in Christ', all the privileges and rights of Christ are made available to him. Then a believer, who has already been incorporated into Christ who is the whole armour of God, can declare boldly, 'I can do all things through Christ who strengthens me' (Phil. 4:13). When believers have put on Christ, He then becomes their source of strength and power to stand against the wiles of the devil.

Again, 'stand' is an imperative; and it is significant for Paul's message. To 'stand' or 'withstand' in verses 11, 13 and 14 is an invitation to vigilance. By the use of these words, Paul is calling the believers to a position of careful defence of their faith. Christ has defeated the powers and principalities. What now remains is for believers to defend the victory Christ has won for them.

In verse 12, Paul reveals the reason for such empowerment:

'For we do not wrestle against flesh and blood, but against principalities, against powers, against the rulers of the darkness of this age, against spiritual hosts of wickedness in the heavenly places.' In what follows we shall discuss Paul's picture of 'the whole armour of God', in the context of spiritual weapons needed to fight the battle of faith.[4]

The girdle of truth: *personal testimony*

As he details what constitutes the 'whole armour of God', Paul begins with the 'girdle of truth'. The girdle was a belt around the Roman soldier's waist which wrapped together the military uniform, keeping his appearance very smart; and making him ready for any given action. One of the functions of the girdle was to fasten the sword to the side of the soldier. The fact that the girdle is located on the waist is significant. The waist under normal circumstance is a point of stability for the body. 'Truth' is what is required to keep believers properly balanced as they continue their journey of faith. This truth is what keeps believers holy, in their encounter with the powers of darkness. Hence, Christ prays for His disciples, 'Sanctify them by Your truth. Your word is truth' (John 17:17).

This is the sense in which the believer's word of testimony becomes an effective weapon of spiritual warfare. In their word of testimony, the truth of what Christ has accomplished for them is proclaimed. The Scripture attests to the effectiveness of this weapon, 'And they overcame him [the dragon]...by the word of their testimony' (Rev. 12:11). What does it mean to overcome by their word of testimony? A testifier is a person who gives an accurate account of what he knows about the deeds of a particular person or an incident that has happened.

In the use of his testimony, a believer rises up to confront the devil about the fact of the sufficiency of the blood of Christ which was shed on the cross at Calvary as the basis for the defeat of the powers of darkness. This blood is also the power that has rescued the believer from the garb of demonic powers. A testimony is an open declaration of truth, and in this case it is the declaration of the fact of the victory of Christ over the powers of darkness, of which the believer is a beneficiary. Having been rescued from the powers of darkness, the believer declares his total allegiance to Christ by putting the devil to shame. This he does by renouncing him publicly.

An essential aspect of this testimony is to expose openly whatever weapons of the dark kingdom that had been in the possession of the believer before being born into the Kingdom of God. This is another way of saying that he declares the truth of his new standing in Christ. In this respect, Paul writes to the Ephesians:

> And have no fellowship with the unfruitful works of darkness, but rather expose them. For it is shameful even to speak of those things which are done by them in secret. But all things that are exposed are made manifest by the light, for whatever makes manifest is light (Eph. 5:11-13).

Rather than putting up with the works of darkness, the believer should publicly expose them. This is what the devil hates to see. He does not like the truth to be told. He is aggressively angry when the secrets of his kingdom are exposed. This was the method used by the new converts in Ephesus, 'And many who had believed came confessing and telling their deeds. Also, many of those who had practised magic brought their books together and burned them in the sight of all' (Acts 19:18-19). Just as it was effective for the total deliverance of believers then, so it is still effective today.

It is dangerous to be a secret disciple. What Satan is interested in doing is to keep a believer in suspense about his new experience in Christ. The devil keeps on suggesting what may happen if the deliverance is not total. He is a specialist in reminding believers about all the negative implications of the *ifs*. When he is threatening them with *his own ifs*, they can equally use the truth of the gospel message to silence him by their *word of testimony*. The way to do this is to remind Satan about the fact of the death and resurrection of Christ, which is not only an assurance of life after death to believers who have died in the faith of Christ, but is also the bedrock of believers' victory over the powers of darkness here on earth. Paul states this clearly:

Now if Christ is preached that He has been raised from the dead, how do some among you say that there is no resurrection of the dead? But if there is no resurrection of the dead, then Christ is not risen. And if Christ is not risen, then our preaching is vain and your faith is also vain. Yes, and we are found witnesses of God, because we have testified of God that He raised up Christ, whom He did not raise up – if in fact the dead do not rise. For if the dead do not rise, then Christ is not risen. And if Christ is not risen, your faith is futile; you are still in your sins [bondage]! Then those who have fallen asleep in Christ have perished. If in this life only we have hope in Christ, we are of all men the most pitiable. But now Christ is risen from the dead, and has become the firstfruits of those who have fallen asleep (1 Cor. 15:12-20).

As a child of God running the race that has been set before you, refuse to be intimidated by the lies of Satan. Refuse to yield to his suggestions that should you testify to what Christ has done for you or should you dare to expose the operations in the kingdom of darkness (to which you previously belonged), your victory would be short-lived. Remember that your victory is a permanent one which Christ has won for you on the cross at Calvary. You have entered into that victory insofar as 'your life is hidden with Christ in God' (Col. 3:3).

The breastplate of righteousness: *the name of Jesus*
The second piece in 'the whole armour of God is the 'breastplate of righteousness' (Eph. 6:14). 'Righteousness' is to be understood in a forensic sense equivalent to 'justification'. Righteousness[5] is God's gift to those who believe in Christ. In other words, to be declared righteous is to be justified. Believers are justified when they confess Jesus Christ as one's personal Lord and Saviour. Thus, the Scripture says, 'if you confess with your mouth the Lord Jesus and believe in your heart that God has raised Him from the dead, you will be saved' (Rom. 10:9). Here 'confession with mouth' and 'believing in heart' should be seen as the two sides of the same coin. That is to say, what the mouth confesses must first of all be established in the heart. What is confessed must flow from the heart. Therefore the heart is the repository of the faith by which the believer has been justified.

To put on the breastplate of righteousness is to keep alive in one's heart the confession of the name of Christ, which is the power that has rescued the believer from the kingdom of darkness. This is another way of saying that the power in the name of Christ must be kept fresh in one's thought to retain the integrity of his faith. If there is any weapon that believers have readily trusted for victory in the times of trouble, it is the power in the name of Jesus. The only qualification that is necessary for the use of this weapon is to have been justified by Him, to 'be in Christ' (2 Cor. 5:17). Consequently, such an individual has the right to use the name of Jesus. In other words, the name of Jesus is not magic; rather it is a supernatural power that brings about victory for those who know Him, and whom He knows: 'I am the good shepherd; and I know My sheep, and am known by My own' (John 10:14).

The powers of darkness know the identity of those who have been given the authority to use the power in name of Jesus to cast out demons (Mark 16:16-18).[6] The name would not work for those who have not been bought with the blood of Christ (1 Cor. 6:20. cf., Eph. 2:12). Therefore when the Jewish exorcists took it upon themselves to cast out evil spirits from the demon possessed, as if calling the name of Christ were a matter of merely usual a magical power by saying, 'We adjure you by the Jesus whom Paul preaches' (Acts 19:13), and not the Jesus they knew themselves, 'the evil spirit answered and said, Jesus I know, and Paul I know; but who are you?' (Acts 19:15). The point is clear; since *righteousness* has not fellowship with *lawlessness* (2 Cor. 6:14), the name of the Lord Jesus will only work for those who have a living relationship with Him.

Christians know that the name of the Lord is a strong tower that they can run to for their defence whenever Satan, like a lion, roars at them. There is no power than can equal the name of Jesus. God has 'given Him the name which is above every name, that at the name of Jesus every knee should bow, of those in heaven, and of those on earth, and of those under the earth' (Phil. 2:9-10).

With the name of Jesus Christ on your lips, you are undisputedly an overcomer. This is a spiritual weapon that is invisible, but yet the results of the exploits it makes are manifestly visible and amazing. Therefore, keep alive your confession of faith as you 'put on the breastplate of righteousness!'

The shield of faith: *resistance of ungodly thoughts*

The acceptance of the offer of the gift of salvation is what has translated believers from the reign of darkness to the kingdom of light (Eph. 2:8-9). Thus, the third weapon for the believer's spiritual warfare is faith. Paul had earlier commended the Ephesians for their genuine faith (1:15), which was the basis of their salvation. But, as he writes here, his use of faith is to be understood from the perspective of trust. Faith here is their trust in Christ to uphold them in the days ahead, just as the author of Hebrews writes, 'Now faith is the substance of things hoped for, the evidence of things not seen' (Heb. 11:1). Faith is to believe what you do not see, and its reward is to receive what you believe. The Christian life is a life of faith. It is to believe moment by moment in the power that is able to save to the uttermost:

> Now to Him who is able to keep you from stumbling, and to present you faultless before the presence of His glory with exceeding joy, to God our Saviour, who alone is wise, be glory and majesty, dominion and power, both now and forever. Amen (Jude verses 24-25).

If there is anything that Satan aims at doing, it is to destroy the believer's faith, knowing that if he succeeds in destroying his faith, he has succeeded in destroying the kernel of his Christian life.

It is by faith that believers know that the forces of darkness are not genuine powers. It is by faith they know that the powers of darkness have been conquered and defeated. By faith they know that Satan may roar like a lion, but he is not the lion. Jesus Christ is the *only Lion* of the tribe of Judah (Rev. 5:5). In other words, faith must be preserved. It must be nurtured and kept alive on a regular basis if any redeemed Christian will stay in victory. The best way to nurture this faith is by meditating on the Word of God regularly.

Faith keeps believers in obedience to God under every circumstance. While the devil is capitalising on what can be seen physically to make them doubt the reality of God, or the relevance of His promise to them, their faith can answer the devil by telling him that they walk not by sight but by faith. By faith they can call into existence those things which are not as if they were (Rom. 4:17). That is why Paul referred to faith as a 'shield'. With this shield, believers on a regular basis 'will be able to quench all fiery darts of the wicked one' (Eph. 6:16). Forces of darkness are regularly shooting their arrows – the fiery darts to kill. But when a believer is armed with the shield of faith, he shall 'not be afraid…of the arrow that flies by the day' (Ps. 91:5). Our faith has a significant role to play to keep us from falling victim to the devil.

Satan will not stop raging against the saints of God. That is why he walks to and fro on the face of the earth looking for his prey (Job 1:7; cf. 1 Pet. 5:8). The forces of darkness are extremely dangerous. We cannot overcome them in our own strength. What can face and conquer them is the shield of faith rooted in the Word of God. For Paul, the shield is large enough to provide total protection for the believers. O'Brien describes this shield:

> The shield referred to is not the small round one which left most of the body unprotected, but the large shield carried by Roman soldiers, which covered the whole person…. The large shield used by the Roman soldiers was specially designed to quench dangerous missiles, particularly arrows that were dipped in pitch and lit before being fired.[8]

In Satan's attempt to lure them back into his kingdom, believers should learn to exercise their faith, using it to counter-attack any wiles coming from the devil. Peter stresses the usefulness of faith in the face of the ravenous attack of the powers and principalities as he enjoins us to, 'Resist him [the devil], steadfast in faith' (1 Peter 5:9). In other words, faith is an effective weapon at our disposal to put the powers of darkness to flight.

The helmet of salvation: *living in holiness*

Those being addressed by Paul were believers in Christ. Thus for Paul, the fourth weapon of spiritual warfare is 'the helmet of salvation'. With the deliverance of an unbeliever from the powers of darkness, a new creation has been born into the kingdom of

God. An addition has been made into the family of God. However, this impartation of new life is not the end of the new experience, rather the race in the Christian faith has just begun. The new Christian is to contend for the faith that has been handed over to him (Jude 3). For new converts, the lives of mature Christians are worthy of emulation, since they are bringing honour to God. But new converts must be informed that these mature Christians have learned to fight the battle of faith with spiritual weapons.

Now that the seed sown (the Word of God) has germinated, there are two reasons why it is imperative to water it regularly for quality growth. First, Satan will try to make the new convert to be like the seed that fell on the rocky surface with a little depth of soil, that only survived for a short time, and which because 'it had no root it withered away' (Mark 4:5-6). Secondly, Satan may want the new convert to be like the seed that fell among the thorns (Mark 4:18-19), so he will surround him with a lot of side attractions, so much so that he will soon find it difficult to give proper attention to the Word of God that can shield him from the attack of the enemy, .

In the light of these two dangers, what Christians need is sound biblical teaching where they are exposed to the solid food of the Word (1 Pet. 2:2). Hence, Paul admonishes them to 'take the helmet of salvation' (Eph. 6:17). The head must be protected in order for the whole body to remain healthy. In the head lies the centre of intellectual activities, the centre of reasoning. But in addition to this, there are vital organs that are attached to the head that must be presented as living sacrifice to the Lord if the believer is to maintain his spiritual sanity. Three of these will receive attention below.

First is the *eye*. The two eyes must be consecrated to the Lord to keep them away from being the gateway to spiritual disaster. The first organ to be seized by Satan for his use is the eye as he carries out his onslaught against humanity. He is always dangling ungodly scenes before believers. These are coated with deceit to make them fall victims. In the garden of Eden, he told Eve that by eating the forbidden fruit her 'eyes will be opened' (Gen. 3:5). Consequently, 'the woman saw that the tree was good for food, that it was pleasant to the eyes' (Gen. 3:6). The eyes were also responsible for the double sins of David, adultery in the first instance, and subsequently murder.

> Then it happened one evening that David arose from his bed and walked on the roof of the king's house. And from the roof he saw a woman bathing, and the woman was very beautiful to behold. Then David sent messengers, and took her; and she came to him, and he lay with her (2 Sam. 11:2, 4).

So also does the Scripture say in the first epistle of John, 'For all that is in the world – the lust of the flesh, the lust of the eyes, and the pride of life – is not of the Father but is of the world (1 John 2:16). Job knows the dangers to which the eyes are prone as he writes; 'I have made a covenant with my eyes; why then should I look upon a young woman?' (Job 31:1). Thus, the eyes must be tamed and kept away from beholding vain things.

The second organ attached to the head is the *ear*. The two ears must be closed to hearing ungodly words. Instead, they must be kept open, listening to God and what He has to say in such a way that believers would be able to respond at the right time saying, 'Speak Lord, for Your servant hears' (1 Sam. 3:10).

The third organ is the *mouth*, which must be used to tell forth the glory of God. The mouth of a believer must be filled with the good news that will gladden the hearts of those around him. It must always be employed in the task of blessing and not cursing (Rom. 12:14), as the same source cannot produce both 'fresh and bitter water' (Jam. 3:11).

Indeed, the head must be properly protected with the 'helmet of salvation' so as to prevent Satan from taking advantage of its exposure to ungodly seeing of the eyes or to unprofitable news filtering to the ears or to coarse jestings issuing out of the mouth.

The sword of the Spirit: *the word of God*
The fifth spiritual weapon essential for spiritual warfare is the *word of God*. The 'word of God' can be understood in two ways. First, it can be interpreted to mean the contents of the gospel message, the good news about the benefits of the life, ministry, death and

resurrection of Christ. This is the bedrock of salvation. This is the apostolic content that Paul had preached to the Corinthians:

> For I delivered to you first of all that which I also received: that Christ died for our sins according to the Scriptures, and that He was buried, and that He rose again the third day according to the Scriptures' (1 Cor. 15:3-4).

Secondly, the word of God can also be used to cover the entire Scriptures. In this sense, it refers both to the Old and New Testaments. The words of Paul in 2 Timothy 3:15-17 clearly bring this out:

> And that from childhood you have known the Holy Scriptures, which are able to make you wise for salvation through faith which is in Christ Jesus. All Scripture is given by inspiration of God, and is profitable for doctrine, for reproof, for correction, for instruction in righteousness, that the man of God may be complete, thorough equipped for every good work.

For the purpose of this section, the word of God will be considered from the broad perspective of the whole of the Scriptures.

In the view of Paul, 'the weapons of our warfare are not carnal but mighty through God to the pulling down of strongholds' (2 Cor. 10:4).[9] One stronghold of the devil is the mind of man. This is the area that controls the thinking of every human being, whether Christian or non-Christian. What makes the difference in the life of a believer is that his mind, which once used to be the seat of wicked thoughts, has now been taken over by godly thoughts. This is where the word of God is so important. 'Let the word of Christ dwell in you richly in all wisdom, teaching and admonishing one another in psalms and hymns and spiritual songs, singing with grace in your hearts to the Lord' (Col. 3:16).

Paul calls the word of God 'the sword of the Spirit' (Eph. 6:17). The author of the epistle to the Hebrews describes in apt manner the effectiveness of the word of God as the sword of the Spirit in the believers' fight against the unseen powers of the dark kingdom. 'For the word of God is living and powerful, and sharper than any two-edged sword, piercing even to the division of soul and spirit, and of joints and marrow, and is a discerner of the thoughts and intents of the heart' (Heb. 4:12).

Satan's main pre-occupation concerning believers is to keep on offering many tantalising suggestions to them. Of course, they are not bound to accept any suggestions filtering into their minds from the devil. If their minds are saturated with the word of God, they will be able to discern the hands of the enemy at work. They will be able to use relevant passages of Scripture to counter his offensive attack.

If the devil suggests to a believer the thoughts of adultery, the Christian needs to throw at him immediately the sword of the Spirit: 'Do you not know that your bodies are members of Christ? Shall I then take the members of Christ and make them members of a harlot? Certainly not' (1 Cor. 6:15).

Perhaps after a Christian has been rescued from the web of satanic kingdom, his financial situation may become worse. Satan might suggest that the believer should try the devil's own methods and get rich quickly? The Christian can destroy the suggestion with the sword of the Spirit that it is only God 'who gives power to make wealth' (Deut. 8:18), therefore 'though He slay me, yet will I trust Him' (Job 13:15). In other words, he can tell the devil that financial loss will not make him go back to the kingdom of darkness.

It may even happen that after deliverance from the kingdom of darkness, a misfortune comes along – loss of vehicle, death of loved ones, loss of job or a terrible sickness. Such instances may provide opportunities for the devil to try to lure believers back into his den. But as children of God, who are soaked in the word of God, they can put the devil to shame by reminding him that Christ does not promise a life free of trouble. In confidence they can declare the promise of Christ and claim the same to the shame of Satan: 'In the world you will have tribulation; but be of good cheer, I have overcome the world' (John 16:33b). Thus, since Christ has overcome, the believer is also an overcomer, regardless of the tricks of the devil. No matter how terrible the situation they are passing through, the word of God, when used appropriately, will bring the comfort of the Holy Spirit and also put the devil to shame.

The point of emphasis here is that believers need to grow in the

word of God. It is the spiritual sword that they need to fight the
unseen battles. It is not enough for them to be delivered from the
kingdom of darkness; they must ensure that they are not drawn
back into its bondage. It is not a matter of pleading with the enemy
to leave them alone. He does not understand that soft language.
They must fight back with the sword of the Spirit, which is the
word of God.

The secret of the whole armour: *the power of prayer*
Paul knows the power that is in prayer. Regularly he was found
appealing to his converts to pray for him for one thing or another
(Col. 3:3). It may be argued that prayer cannot be regarded as part
of the 'whole armour' since the other parts are described
metaphorically. Nevertheless, we will present prayer as *the invisible
part of the armour*, which knits together in the spiritual realm *the
various parts of the whole armour*. Viewed from this perspective,
the sixth weapon of spiritual warfare is prayer. Prayer is the hottest
spiritual weapon that keeps the forces of darkness in chains and
from invading the presence of Christians. The moment a Christian
goes on his knees to pray, Satan is in trouble.

The ministry of Jesus Christ was rooted in prayer. Regularly
He went apart to be alone with the Father in prayer (Luke 6:12).
He knew the importance of prayer, and so commanded His disciples
in a parable 'that men always ought to pray and not lose heart'
(Luke 18:1). Towards the end of His ministry Jesus Christ equally
warned the disciples to 'Watch and pray, lest you enter into
temptation' (Matt. 26:41). In the same way Paul urges his
congregations to indulge in the habit of regular prayer. To the
Thessalonians he writes, 'Pray without ceasing' (I Thess. 5:17).

When we develop an attitude of praying regularly our spiritual
lives will be richer, deeper and fuller. We will be well fortified to
face many challenges coming from the kingdom of darkness. But
Satan knows the effectiveness of this spiritual weapon, so what he
does is to cause Christians to develop a sense of apathy about prayer.
What happens then is that they lose spiritual vitality, become dry
and weak, and consequently lose spiritual power. This is why Satan
is working vigorously against Christians to ensure that they become

too busy to spend quality time in prayer and communion with God. Yes, *a prayer-less Christian is a power-less Christian.*

The statement of the Lord Jesus Christ in Matthew 17:19-21 on the inability of His disciples to cast out the demonic spirit from the son of a certain man brought to them is highly indicative of the premium He places on the effectiveness of prayer as a spiritual weapon:

> Then the disciples came to Jesus privately and said, 'Why could we not cast him out?' So Jesus said to them, 'Because of your unbelief; for assuredly, I say to you, if you have faith as a mustard seed, you will say to this mountain, "Move from here to there," and it will move; and nothing will be impossible for you. However, this kind does not go out except by *prayer* and fasting.'

It is quite evident that prayer is a powerful spiritual weapon to dislodge Satan of his stronghold on the life of human beings.

By implication also, *a prayerful Christian is a powerful Christian.* If you want to see the chains of the powers of darkness regularly broken, then pray without ceasing in the attitude of praise and thanksgiving. Your prayer must rise up beyond the level of complaint, to that of real fellowship with God, as was the case with Paul and Silas in the book of the Acts:

> But at midnight Paul and Silas were praying and singing hymns to God, and the prisoners were listening to them. Suddenly there was a great earthquake, so that the foundations of the prison were shaken; and immediately all the doors were opened and everyone's chains were loosed (Acts 16:25-26).

The kind of prayer that is effective enough to be a spiritual weapon to cause a destabilisation in the kingdom of darkness is not mere routine prayer. We are not talking about mechanical prayer that lacks spiritual substance. This form of prayer is not the one in which your mind wanders away while you are on your knees; nor is it the one where you dose off, easily losing your concentration in the course of praying, as was the case with the disciples in the Garden of Gethsemane (Matt. 26:40, 43). It was not surprising that the disciples became easy prey for the devil, 'Then all the disciples forsook Him and fled' (Matt. 26:56). Of special attention was the prayerless Peter, who went on to deny Christ three times (Matt. 26:70, 72, 74).

Prayer that is strong enough to be an effective spiritual weapon must be Spirit-saturated and directed. It must be prayer that enables one to gaze at the glory of God, at Jesus Christ His Son, and on His finished work on the cross at Calvary (Acts 7:55, 60). Though it is the Spirit that helps us to pray (Rom. 8:26), yet we must make ourselves available for Him to use. We must be ready vessels through whom the Holy Spirit can make intercession. The Holy Spirit will not force Himself on anybody for the purpose of prayer, but will readily come in to those who make themselves available to Him. This is for the purpose of engaging in serious battle against the powers and principalities. Yes, for forces of darkness to be demobilised on a permanent basis, it is essential to pray 'always with all prayer and supplication in the Spirit' (Eph. 6:18).

One other thing that prayer does for believers is that it equips them to be able to witness effectively. Satan's intention is always to prevent the spread of the good news of the gospel. He is always doing this since he knows that this is the means by which his kingdom is regularly torn apart when unbelievers and those in bondage to his powers are rescued. Paul is not ignorant of this fact (1 Thess. 2:18). He writes to the Ephesians: 'And [pray] for me, that utterance may be given to me, that I may open my mouth boldly to make known the mystery of the gospel, for which I am an ambassador in chains, that in it I may speak boldly, as I ought to speak' (Eph. 6:19-20).

Indeed, prayer is needful for effective preaching of the gospel. To preach the good news is synonymous with taking the battle to the danger zones, the enemies' territories. For the gates of hell not to prevail in the process of preaching the good news, prayer to God for boldness and courage is a must. If there are believers who have learnt to defeat the powers of darkness in the process of preaching the gospel message, they are those who have learnt the secret of prayer. The experience of Peter and John in the book of Acts bears witness to this fact:

And they [the chief priests and the elders] called them [Peter and John] and commanded them not to speak at all nor teach in the name of Jesus.... So when they heard that, they [believers] raised their voice to God with one accord and said....'Now, Lord, look on their threats, and grant to Your servants that with boldness they may speak Your word, by stretching our Your hand to heal, and that signs and wonders may be done through the name of Your holy Servant Jesus.' And when they had prayed, the place where they were assembled together was shaken; and they were all filled with the Holy Spirit, and they spoke the word of God with boldness (Acts 4:18, 24, 29-31).

The result of their prayer was amazing. The text reveals two outstanding phenomena that followed. First, 'they were all filled with the Holy Spirit.' The Holy Spirit is the power that a believer needs to preach the message of the gospel. Thus, in addition to the initial empowerment on the Day of Pentecost (Acts 2:2-4), Peter and John, and of course the other apostles, were again refilled with the power of the Holy Spirit in a greater dimension. In other words, they were recharged for greater exploits over the kingdom of darkness. Believers need to pray regularly, asking God for fresh anointings of the Holy Spirit to be able to preach the good news.

Secondly, after that prayer, 'they spoke the word of God with boldness.' The prayer offered had connected the apostles to the heavenly source of power that they needed to minister. Hence, the Spirit of boldness in them overshadowed the spirit of fear (2 Tim. 1:7). Therefore they were able to proclaim the message without minding what the powers of darkness could do, simply because they knew that greater is He who is in them than the devil who is in the world (1 John 4:4). Not even the powers and principalities operating through their agents, namely 'the priests, the captains of the temple, and the Sadducees' (Acts 4:1), could match the power of God in them. Believers need to declare the good news of what Christ has done in their lives. This is by way of telling forth the good news of the arrival of the kingdom of God in their new experience of salvation. But for them to do this, they must have learnt the secret of prayer.

Conclusion

As we bring our discussion in this chapter to a close, it is necessary to remind ourselves about the reality of the ongoing battle for every sincere believer. Just as the forces of darkness are vigorously pursuing young Christians to bring them back into the dark kingdom, likewise mature Christians are under demonic surveillance. However, no matter the aggressive moves of the devil in this spiritual warfare, believers should not fret, but rather they should rejoice knowing that although the battle is fierce, the Captain of their salvation is with them (Matt. 28:20).

With this great assurance, let all believers at whatever stage of the Christian faith 'lay aside every weight, and the sin which so easily ensnares us, and let us run with endurance the race that is set before us, looking unto Jesus, the author and finisher of our faith' (Heb. 12:1-2). He is the Jehovah Nissi, the Lord our Banner (Exod. 17:15). Therefore, the battle is not ours, but the Lord's. Hence, 'When the enemy [Satan] comes in like a flood, the Spirit of the Lord will lift up a standard against him' (Isa. 59:19).

9

The Purpose of Victory in Spiritual Warfare

When the powers of darkness encounter the Power of God, who is Jesus Christ (1 Cor. 1:24), they completely collapse and Satan's flaunted powers are stripped-off. The obvious way that this has been demonstrated is in the total liberation of believers from the powers of darkness. Since all authority has been given to Christ, believers who were once slaves and bound helpless to the dictates of satanic powers have been set free from the captivity of their tormentors. Directly following from this is the fact that these believers, who were instruments of service in the kingdom of darkness, have become instruments of righteousness (Rom. 6:19). What used to be employed by Satan in his wicked services has now been taken over by Christ in His service. So what is the purpose of the victory Christ has won for believers in their spiritual warfare? This purpose will be examined from five angles, in each case bringing out the significance of the new life in Christ.

1. The power of light overshadows darkness
First, the primary purpose of victory in spiritual warfare is to convince unbelievers who are still in bondage to the powers of darkness that *the light shines in the darkness, and the darkness did not comprehend It* (John 1:5). While the power of the gospel message will manifest itself in the salvation of many people as the good news is preached (Acts 17:1-4), yet there are those who will never choose the option of accepting the same message for their salvation. Rather what they will do is to oppose the gospel since they are engrossed in the works of darkness (Acts 17:5).

These people who determine not to accept the message of the gospel must always look for different ways of preventing the further spread of the good news. However, the more they try, the more they come to the realisation of the fact that it is impossible to prevent the spread of the gospel. This undoubtedly is a clear demonstration of the reality of ineffectiveness of their powers, put side by side with the power of God:

> Now when they had passed through Amphipolis and Apollonia, they came to Thessalonica where there was a synagogue of the Jews. Then Paul, as his custom was, went in to them, and for three Sabbaths reasoned with them from the Scripture, explaining and demonstrating that the Christ had to suffer and rise again from the dead, and saying, this Jesus whom I preach to you is the Christ. And some of the men were persuaded; and a great multitude of the devout Greeks, and not few of the leading women, joined Paul and Silas. But the Jews who were not persuaded ...set all the city in an uproar and attacked the house of Jason, and sought to bring them to the people. But when they did not find them, they dragged Jason and some brethren to the rulers of the city, crying out, 'These who have turned the world upside down have come here too.' Then the brethren immediately sent Paul and Silas away by night to Berea. But when the Jews from Thessalonica learned that the word of God was preached by Paul at Berea, they came there also and stirred up the crowd (Acts 17:1-5, 10, 13).

The confession of those evil men of Thessalonica that 'These who have turned the world upside down have come here too' clearly demonstrates their acceptance of a superior power over their own self-willed powers. Even though to them, the power of the gospel was perceived as evil,[1] since it contradicted their wickedness, yet they could not fail to see how the same power meant God's blessing to those who have been changed by the preaching of the good news. Thus, the problem of these wicked men of Thessalonica can be explained in the fact that though they recognised the goodness in the power of the gospel, yet they were still opposed to it. This is the sense in which Patte writes about the dilemma of such an idolatrous system:

> But from the perspective of the idolatrous system of convictions, this same manifestation of God is simultaneously viewed, on the one hand, as 'evil' and thus as nondivine or even antidivine and, on the other hand, as divine, good and blessing.[2]

The fact is that these evil men have recognised the truth, but to accept the truth was the problem they were struggling with. The harder they tried to sweep the truth under the carpet, the more it surfaced and caught up with them. Therefore what the victory of the power of God seeks to demonstrate in spiritual warfare is the fact that there is nothing the power of darkness can do to hinder the spread of the good news. The forces of darkness know this and against their wish they often declare the supremacy of this power, having come face-to-face in encounter with it:

> And when He stepped out on the land, there met Him a certain man from the city who had demons for a long time. And he wore no clothes, nor did he live in a house but in the tombs. When he saw Jesus, he cried out, fell down before Him, and with a loud voice said, 'What have I to do with You, Jesus, Son of the Most High God? I beg You, do not torment me!' (Luke 8:28).

Again, the victory of the power of God over the powers of Baal in the contest on Mount Carmel is the fact of light shining forth in the darkness, without the powers of darkness being able to overcome it:

> So Ahab sent for all the children of Israel, and gathered the prophets together on Mount Carmel. And Elijah came to all the people, and said, 'How long will you falter between two opinions? If the LORD is God, follow Him; but if Baal, then follow him.' But the people answered him not a word.... Now Elijah said to the prophets of Baal, 'Choose one bull for yourselves and prepare it first, for you are many; and call on the name of your god, but put no fire under it. Then call on the name of your gods, and I will call on the name of the LORD; and the God who answers by fire, He is God.' And the people answered and said, 'It is well spoken'.... So they took the bull which was given them, and they prepared it, and called on the name of Baal from morning even till noon, saying, 'O Baal, hear us!' But there was no voice; no one answered....And it came to pass, at the time of the offering of the evening sacrifice, that Elijah the prophet came near and said, 'LORD God of Abraham, Isaac, and Israel, let it be known this day that You are God in Israel, and that I am Your servant, and that I have done all these at Your word. Hear me, O LORD, hear me, that this people may know that You have turned their hearts back to You again.' Then the fire of the LORD fell and consumed the burnt sacrifice, and the wood and the stones and the dust, and it licked up

the water that was in the trench. Now when all the people saw it, they fell on their faces; and they said, 'The LORD, He is God! The LORD, He is God!' (1 Kings 18:20-26, 36-39).

This was a contest between the kingdom of God and the kingdom of darkness, at the end of which the powers of darkness acknowledged the supremacy of the power of God. The fact that 'they fell on their faces' was a true acknowledgement of the only living God. However, this was not enough for the powers and principalities to surrender to the sovereign rule of God, for king Ahab and his wife Jezebel vowed to snuff the life out of Elijah:

> And Ahab told Jezebel all that Elijah had done, also how he had executed all the prophets with the sword. Then Jezebel sent a messenger to Elijah, saying, 'So let the gods do to me, and more also, if I do not make you life as the life of one of them by tomorrow about this time' (1 Kings 19:1-2).

With the execution of the prophets of Baal, who could be regarded as agents of darkness insofar as they were working in partnership with the demonic monarchical institution, Jezebel was enraged. She threatened to kill a prophet of God. Again, the threat of Jezebel was a mere *roaring* of the devil who like a lion seeks whom to devour (1 Pet. 5:8). The execution of Elijah was an impossible task for the kingdom of darkness to accomplish unless God would allow it. Therefore, the victory of believers in spiritual warfare is an open testimonial to the fact of the powerlessness of the forces of the dark kingdom when they come in a face-to-face encounter with the power of God.

2. Stand firm in the liberty

While Christ, the power of God, has rescued the victims of the dark kingdom from the oppressive reign of Satan, such liberty is not to be taken for granted. Thus, secondly, for victory in spiritual warfare to continue, believers need to be warned of the dangers associated with spiritual lethargy and the consequence of backsliding into their former ungodly way of life. They must not think of continuing in sin and expect the grace of God to abound in their lives (Rom. 6:1-2). Though salvation is free for each believer in Christ, it is not cheap. While this rescue operation has cost them nothing, it has cost God His best, the gift of 'His only begotten Son' (John 3:16) who has purchased the release of believers with his precious blood (1 Cor. 6:20). Therefore warning believers of the dangers of backsliding, the author of Hebrews writes:

> Now the just [those who have already been delivered from the powers of darkness] shall live by faith; but if anyone draws back, My soul has no pleasure in him. But we are not of those who draw back to perdition, but of those who believe to the saving of the soul (Heb. 10:38-39).

There are a few important points to note from the above passage. First, it is required that those who have been rescued from demonic powers are expected to put their faith into action on a moment-by-moment basis. What can keep them to the end of the race, to be able to say like Paul that, 'I fought the good fight, I have finished the race' (2 Tim. 4:7), is a daily life of absolute faith in the finished work of Christ on the cross. In other words, the purpose of victory in spiritual battle is to remind believers of where they have been rescued from, and of the need to guard the instrument of their salvation – *their faith* in Christ (Gal. 2:20). Their salvation is not to be taken for granted. Salvation must not be seen as a licence for unguarded living. Hence Paul writes to the Galatians, 'Stand fast therefore in the liberty by which Christ has made us free, and do not be entangled again with the yoke of bondage' (Gal. 5:1).

While for the Galatians, their own yoke of bondage in the context of the law could either be circumcision, observance of dietary regulations or the keeping of certain special days (Gal. 2:11-12, 4:10), for the Ephesians, and of course Africans who have been delivered from the kingdom of darkness in the context of our present discussion, their own yoke of bondage will be a return to the practice of witchcraft, of magic, the use of charms, and enlistment in the membership of secret cults (cf. Acts 19:18-19). Going back to any of these is to be entangled again with the yoke of bondage and, indeed, a re-enactment of the broken covenant with Satan. It must be avoided!

The second point to note from Hebrews 10:38-39 is that God is not pleased with any saved soul who draws back from the commonwealth of believers. Why? Because such an action amounts to heading towards perdition. For such, there may not be any time for further rescue operations. Satan is ever on the look out, always alert, looking for the slightest opportunity so that believers can make a shipwreck of their faith. The reason for this is to deal the final blow on them, which will not only kill them, but also destroy them eternally (John 10:10). He is always looking for the chance to bring eternal damnation to saved souls. Indeed, like a roaring lion, he roams about seeking whom to devour (1 Pet. 5:8).

Going back into the kingdom of darkness will mean perdition in all its ramifications. It is only right that, once a believer is rescued from the kingdom of darkness, he should see his victory as God's call upon his life to remain in the safety zone. No wonder, Jesus warned the man who was previously in bondage to the spirit of lameness for 38 years to remain in that safety zone of salvation and healing, otherwise a greater calamity might befall him. 'Afterward Jesus found him in the temple, and said to him, 'See, you have been made well. Sin no more, lest a worse thing come upon you' (John 5:14).[3] Therefore for believers, victory in spiritual warfare is an exposure of the wickedness of the kingdom of darkness. They must not go there again so that a worse thing will not come upon them.

Even though we have noted that, for an African, the previous experience in the kingdom of darkness from which deliverance is sought was not viewed primarily as a sin issue, yet in the long run the underling factor can be seen as sin. This is simply because every work of darkness is opposed to the divine command of God (Exod. 20:1-6). In the light of the above, deliverance from the dark kingdom is deliverance from any partnership with the works of darkness. Therefore the purpose of victory in spiritual warfare is to tell the rescued believers that everything that connects to the kingdom of darkness is sinful. Every previous association with forces of darkness is against the will of God. All the practices of the former life before one came to faith in Christ were sinful deeds. Thus, the ultimate purpose of victory in spiritual warfare is to call believers' attention to the fact of sin as an instrument of perdition. As a result, there is the need to always run away from sin.

3. Believers as a demonstration of the power of Christ

Thirdly, believers' victory in spiritual warfare is to demonstrate that Christians are people of power. Their power is derived from the power of Christ Himself who says, 'Most assuredly, I say to you, he who believes in Me, the works that I do he will do also; and greater works than these he will do, because I go to My Father' (John 14:12). Just as they recognised Jesus Christ while He was here physically on earth, in the present dispensation the powers of darkness also recognise that believers are endued with much stronger power than that of the dark kingdom. No wonder, Peter, who was to the unbelieving Jews an 'uneducated and untrained' man (Acts 4:13), could speak authoritatively, when he had been empowered by the Holy Spirit, commanding the spirit of lameness to get out of the man seated at the Beautiful Gate in Jerusalem (Acts 3:6).

Indeed, believers have not received the spirit of fear, but of power and of love and of a sound mind (2 Tim. 1:7). Christians are not ordinary people. They are special people. They are people of destiny and purpose. They are people on whom God has bestowed His special favour (1 Pet. 2:9). They might have been previously clothed with fear and timidity, but once they have been rescued by Jesus Christ they are a manifestation of the power of God wherever they go.[4]

What makes the difference between the former timid Peter and the new bold Peter? It was the presence of Christ in Him. He was in Christ, and Christ was in Him. Peter had been endued with power from on high (Acts 2:1-4). This is a sure confirmation of the truth of the Scripture that 'Jesus is the way the truth and the life' (John 14:6). If He is the truth, it means that He cannot lie. He has said that whatever works He did, whoever believes in Him would do.

Believers are very much engaged now in deliverance ministry. They have been commanded by Christ to be involved in it, to make a consistent onslaught against the kingdom of darkness. Believers must rise up and take their rightful place in this ministry of the church. Christ has bestowed the gift on all believers. It must be used to announce to the kingdom of darkness that believers are people of power already endued by Christ Himself. Shortly before His ascension, Christ assured the apostles:

> But you shall receive power when the Holy Spirit has come upon you; and you shall be witnesses to Me in Jerusalem, and in all Judea and Samaria, and to the end of the earth' (Acts 1:8).

God has given *the right* to every believer who *is in Christ* to make exploit of the kingdom of darkness. 'But as many as received Him, to them He gave the right to become children of God, even to those who believed in His name' (John 1:12). In the binding and casting out of the powers of darkness from those who are in bondage to them, believers are only confirming the truth of the gospel that Jesus Christ is still very much at work in our own generation. Indeed this 'Jesus Christ is the same yesterday, today and forever' (Heb. 13:8). Through His accredited agents, Christ continues to disarm the principalities and powers, making an open show of them and triumphing over their operations in whatever way they seek to keep humanity in bondage.

4. Assurance of the final defeat of the powers of darkness
In chapter 5 we saw how the cross of Christ became the ultimate judgement upon the forces of darkness. Therefore, the fourth purpose of victory in spiritual warfare is to establish the certainty of the final defeat of the powers of darkness. In the crucifixion of Christ, which the rulers of this age thought was their clever agenda to scheme out Christ from the scene of the world events, He defeated all demonic forces operating through these rulers and rendered them powerless. He made a public show of them in His death, and consequently in His resurrection. In the light of the above, Christ was presented in chapter 7 as the Power of God that delivered believers from the bondage of Satan.

Though Christ has delivered us from the powers of darkness, yet as noted in chapter 8 the battle is not yet over. There is the need to keep on fighting in our onward march to the Promised Land. In other words, the present victory of believers anticipates the final victory at the second coming of Christ. That is why believers can still weep because of the death of the loved ones (1 Thess. 4:13). Also, this is why there is still further depreciation of our 'earthly house, this tent' (2 Cor. 5:1). In a sense, Satan is still given a measure of freedom to operate in the present age. He still has a limited authority to act.

Though Satan may still be able to move to and fro on the face of the earth (Job 2:2), however, he is no longer the master. He has been tamed and brought in subjection to the authority of Christ forever. While in spite of his defeat Satan still breathes threats against believers (1 Pet. 5:8), the ultimate plan of God is to wipe out, at the close of the age, every trace of the operation of satanic forces. That is when believers will stand in absolute liberty, free from any further harassment from demonic powers. Then there will be no more spiritual battles to fight. God's divine Kingdom will be permanently established. Therefore, for believers, victory in spiritual warfare is an assurance of the final defeat of Satan and the inheritance of a blessed eternity awaiting them at the second coming of Christ, when they will be gathered to reign with Him eternally.

If Christ, by His death and resurrection, has demonstrated His conquest of the powers of darkness, this victory also is meant to re-assure believers that He will, as a matter of certainty, execute final judgement on the powers and principalities at the close of the age. In the view of Paul, that is the end of all spiritual warfare for believers. 'Then comes the end, when He delivers the kingdom to God the Father, when He puts an end to all rule and all authority and power' (1 Cor. 15:24). The book of Revelation is a picturesque of this final victory, a glance in the present time to the anticipated glory in the future. Thus in the words of Ladd:

> The last book of the New Testament stands in this same stream of interpreted history and looks forward to the consummation of what God had done in Jesus, promising the final destruction of evil and the creation of a new heaven and a new earth when the entire history of God's self-revelation will achieve its divinely intended goal of a perfect human society dwelling in undisturbed fellowship with God.[5]

In the mean time, Satan may continue with his harassment, but the final battle line has been drawn when his activities will be permanently called to a halt. The language of Paul in 1 Corinthians 15:24 is significant; hence we must pay special attention to it. The three words, *rule, authority* and *power* are to be understood from the perspective of our present discussion as 'forces of darkness'.

As noted earlier in chapter 4, the forces of darkness are constantly manifesting their presence in the operations of human agents working in opposition to the divine rulership of God. Thus for believers, victory in spiritual warfare has a uniqueness which goes beyond the present existence in which Satan, though defeated, is still vested with a measure of authority. Each victory is indicative of the certainty of the second coming of Christ when Satan and his cohorts will cease to show their presence where the children of God are gathered.

5. Victory calls for service

The fifth purpose of victory in spiritual warfare is to serve the Lord. Having been declared victorious in spiritual warfare, believers have been given a rare privilege to experience the grace of God. This privilege carries with it the responsibility to serve the Lord. Believers who are now 'new creations' in Christ were once in the services of Satan, doing all that was pleasing to him. But having been freed from the shackles of the enemy, they are now to expend their God-given strength serving the Lord (Rom. 6:22). Thus in the words of Paul, believers are co-workers with Christ (2 Cor. 6:1). In other words, believers are saved to serve.

The Scripture is very instructive on this fact. When God gives any privilege, He equally adds a responsibility to it. He does not want His children to be a mere *Dead Sea*, which always receives in water without giving any out. Therefore freedom from the kingdom of darkness means service in the kingdom of light, the church of God. An example that readily comes to mind in this direction was Mary Magdalene, from whom Jesus Christ cast out seven demonic spirits, and others who were beneficiaries of the grace of God.

> Now it came to pass, afterward, that He [Jesus] went through every city and village, preaching and bringing the glad tidings of the kingdom of God. And the twelve were with Him, and certain women who had been healed of evil spirits and infirmities – Mary called Magdalene, out of whom had come seven demons, and Joanna the wife of Chuza, Herod's steward, and Susanna, and many others who provided for Him from their substance (Luke 8:2).

After the release of Mary Magdalene and others from the kingdom of darkness, they, in gratitude to God for the privilege of their salvation, immediately started ministering to the needs of Christ. Call to service after being delivered from the kingdom of darkness is of various degrees. The essential purpose of this is to enable believers to 'do business till Christ comes' (Luke 19:13). We may ask, 'What business does He want them to do?' The Scripture gives an answer to this question. From the account in Luke we read:

> Now so it was that after three days they found Him in the temple, sitting in the midst of the teachers, both listening to them and asking them questions. And all who heard Him were astonished at His understanding and answers. So when they saw Him, they were amazed; and His mother said to Him, 'Son, why have You done this to us? Look, Your father and I have sought you anxiously.' And He said to them, 'Why is it that you sought Me? Did you not know that I must be about *My Father's business*?' (Luke 2:46-49).

From the above, it must not be construed as if Jesus was displaying any act of rudeness to His parents. Far from it! Rather, He was re-focusing the attention of Joseph and Mary on the fact that He had come into the world at the instance of God (His Father) for a specific purpose. Therefore, nothing must stand in His way. It is evident that the primary business of Christ is the preaching of the good news about the arrival of the Kingdom of God. From Jordan to Golgotha, this was his main preoccupation. Jesus started the business by saying, 'The Spirit of the Lord is upon Me, because He has anointed Me to preach the gospel' (Luke 4:18, cf. Mark 1:15), and concluded the business by saying, 'It is finished' (John 19:30).

In the light of the above, it is clear that the main business of a believer is the preaching of the good news about the arrival of the Kingdom of God. A believer is to serve primarily as an *evangelist*. Herein comes the need for him or her to 'shod [his or her] feet with the preparation of the gospel of peace' (Eph. 6:15).[6] Anybody rescued by the power of God has a unique story to tell, a unique story of his encounter with Christ, who made everything new for him. An evangelist is a person who brings the good news of the kingdom of God to those who are still in the kingdom of darkness. For believers, the purpose of victory in spiritual warfare is that we who have been delivered from the kingdom of darkness should witness to the power of the gospel to save.

This is why testimony is an integral part of the preaching of the gospel message among the African Christians. There are two parts to a testimony. First, a testifier gives a vivid account of his misery and hopelessness while in bondage to the powers of darkness, a situation that prompts him to seek greater power for deliverance. Secondly, he testifies to the overwhelming joy of the Lord in his life now that Christ has delivered him from the powers of darkness, and goes on to encourage others that what Christ has done in his life He is able to do in the lives of those who are still in bondage to the powers of darkness.

When believers, having been delivered from the powers of darkness, and who now radiate the beauty of God on their faces, go out into their immediate environment to 'do business', unbelievers will seek to know the Deliverer who has brought such a change to their lives. In a way, believers will become a life epistle, 'known and read by all men' (2 Cor. 3:2). Having been delivered by the power of God, one must not become a recluse. The new life must be in active interaction with the immediate environment. The new life of believers in Christ must be so contagious that the magicians, cultists, inventors of charms, witches and wizards around them must be able to say, 'These who have turned the world upside down have come here too' (Acts 17:6). But more importantly they will be able to say, 'Men and brethren, what shall we do to be saved?' (Acts 2:37).

Africans know that every act of victory in spiritual warfare is an opportunity to testify to the power of the gospel. From their experience in the dark kingdom, they know that the best way to keep their victory is by telling the good news of their rescue operation on a regular basis. Believers, after being rescued from the powers and principalities, cannot afford to keep the good news to themselves. What God through Christ has done in their lives must be expressed boldly. This is the proclamation of the good news that is able to rescue those who are still in bondage to the powers of darkness.

Another area where the victory of believer in spiritual warfare could spur him to serve is in the area of *teaching*. This is a noble task for the purpose of equipping the saints, who in turn will be able to minister in the world. There is the need for sound teaching so as to guide believers from going into heresies. Teaching is closely associated with the ministry of a pastor.

The farewell speech of Paul to the elders of Ephesus clearly shows that some of them had assumed the responsibilities of teacher-pastor in the church. Paul charged them: 'Therefore take heed to yourselves and to all the flock, among which the Holy Spirit has made you overseers, to shepherd the church of God which He purchased with His own blood' (Acts 20:28). There are three significant words here denoting 'Church-Pastor relationship.' The words are *flock*, *overseers* and *shepherd*. To be able to shepherd and oversee the flock of God, one must be thoroughly grounded in the Scriptures.

The shepherd or overseer needs the word of God to instruct others correctly. Thus an effective way of serving the Lord is in the area of teaching, searching the Scriptures to expose the lies of the devil through well prepared messages explaining the doctrines of the Christian faith. Hence, Paul instructs Timothy, 'Study to show yourself approved to God, a worker who does not need to be ashamed, rightly dividing the word of truth' (2 Tim. 2:15). The more a believer does this, the more he immerses himself in the word of God, the more difficult for the forces of darkness to lure him away from the truth. Thus as a person serving the Lord in the capacity of a teacher, the believer helps to equip the body of Christ. It is equally important to note that Christ Himself has appointed some to the business of teaching for the purpose of 'equipping of the saints for the work of ministry, for the edifying of the body of Christ' (Eph. 4:11-12).

The point of emphasis in this chapter is that it is not enough for believers to be freed from the powers of darkness; they must be available to serve also. As the adage goes, an idle hand is a ready tool for the devil. Thus, when believers engage themselves in Spirit-filled ministries in the church of God, it will be a constant reminder of their victory both in the past and in ongoing spiritual warfare. The commitment of a believer to the ministries of the church will make it imperative for him to 'study to present himself to God, a worker who does not need to be ashamed' (2 Tim. 2:15).

Conclusion

As we round up our discussion, it is appropriate to sound a note of warning so that any form of misconceptions associated with the foregoing might be dealt with appropriately. There is the temptation to think that our discussion, which has placed emphasis on the power of Christ to guarantee believers' victory at all times, is indirectly offering the good news as the easiest option to avoid suffering or persecution. Nothing can be farther than the truth. The fact of the believers' deliverance from the snare of the enemy will still expose them to the reckless attack of the powers of darkness (1 Pet. 5:8). Their success, health, marriage and business may be threatened, or even be permitted by God to be touched by Satan (Job 1:12; 2:6), but that does not mean God has abandoned them. As long as they have been rooted in the Word of God, believers can quickly discern when the powers of darkness are at work. They may wish that the 'thorn in their flesh' be quickly removed from them, but like Paul, since they are constantly operating in the will of God, they also can hear His soothing voice saying, 'My grace is sufficient for you' (2 Cor. 12:9).

The manifestation of the power of God over and above the operations of the principalities and powers is designed to lead believers to submit to the authority of Christ, the great Deliverer, rather than to convey any wrong message of exploitation. In other words, the manifestation of the power of God in a believer's life is not a means for exploitation as Simon wrongly thought in the book of Acts (Acts 8:18-21).

If there is anything that threatens the integrity of the gospel message in our present generation, it is the erroneous *prosperity message* of the modern day preachers. While I am not in any way against the prosperity of believers, since it is the prerogative of God to bless whomever He wishes to bless, yet we must be cautious not to present the gospel as if its sole objective is to make us comfortable in our position of affluence or that poverty is tantamount to fake spirituality. Hence, Jesus warned, 'Take heed and beware of covetousness, for one's life does not consist in the abundance of the things he possesses' (Luke 12:15).

That prosperity gospel has received an upsurge of attention in the modern day Pentecostal Movements globally is no longer a matter of debate. In the words of Simon Coleman,

> It is known variously as the Faith, Faith Formula, Prosperity, Health and Wealth or Word Movement. [It is] one wing of the global charismatic revival [that] has been particularly successful as well as controversial in recent years.[1]

There is no doubt that prosperity message has become a global phenomenon. In other words, emergence of prosperity gospel on the scene of Christianity has gone beyond the realm of mere speculative ideas. In this direction, the case of the Rhema Bible Church in Randburg, Johannesburg, South Africa, may have epitomised the danger of prosperity gospel that can lead to erroneous teaching of the gospel. As noted by Coleman, 'For prosperous white South Africans, Faith ideas are said to present comforting messages that emphasise the need for order in society and justify the possession of wealth as a sign of divine grace.'[2]

Preachers of the gospel must be careful not to present the gospel message as if the economic recessions of the African countries coupled with the apparent dissatisfaction in the socio-political arena are the propelling forces for seeking the alternative source of power rooted in the Scriptures. The message must be sounded loud and clear that the invitation to accept the Lordship of Christ should not be confused with a call to use the name of Christ for exploitation purposes. Otherwise, there will be no genuine basis for challenging the epistemological worldview of non-Christians to abandon their life drenched in the operations of the powers and principalities. While it is true that God does want His children to prosper physically and materially as their soul prospers (3 John 2), the point must be made clear that the promise of complete deliverance from the powers of darkness, which includes prosperity, does not guarantee freedom from trials and persecution. For Christ Himself has said, 'In the world you will have tribulation; but be of good cheer, I have overcome the world' (John 16:31). This point is succinctly echoed by Barron when he writes:

The promise of prosperity does not free us from trial. In fact, we can expect the devil to attack us all the more as we grow in faith. Serving God can land us in painful situations, much as it landed many of the apostles in jail. But as long as we walk in faith God will deliver and prosper us.[3]

As we bring our discussion to a close, a recapitulation of the major points of interest should be helpful. It has been observed that a simple reading of the creation accounts in Genesis 1 and 2 does not reveal any information about *how* and *when* the angelic beings were created. However, by going further in our reading of some selected passages from the Scriptures, both in the Old and New Testaments (Isa. 14:12-14; Ezek. 28:12-17 and Rev. 12:7-9), we have been able to gather a few pieces of information about the creation of Lucifer and his fall, and consequently the origin of the kingdom of darkness. Therefore, in chapter 1 attention was focused on the Biblical account of the origins of the powers and principalities as an entity in opposition to God and His divine rule. The chapter also looked at the origin of spiritual warfare, an ongoing battle in which the sphere of humanity is the battlefield.

In this work, our aim has been to demonstrate that the epistle to the Ephesians is a product of Paul's contact with the city of Ephesus, and that this contact resulted in the emergence of a new community, a congregation of believers in Christ. Thus, in chapter 2 we looked at the ministry of Paul among the Ephesians, noting the power of the gospel and how his preaching brought about a new experience of salvation among the inhabitants there. That chapter also served as a prelude to the apostle's concept of spiritual warfare in Ephesians 6. Paul does not see the Christian life, or rather the new life in Christ, as a passive one. For Paul, there is the need to fight a Christian fight on a regular basis. In this regard, chapter 3 attempted to address the sources for the development of Paul's distinctive language of the powers and principalities. The purpose of this is to be able to understand his concept of spiritual warfare in Ephesians 6 as the believers' resistance of the powers of the old sinful life seeking to bring them back from the Christian faith, and ultimately to the bondage of Satan.

While Paul was not an idealist, but a pragramatist, he knew

that a tough time awaits believers after their salvation experience, even when it has become apparent that they have been crucified with Christ (Gal. 2:20). Paul clearly acknowledged this as he writes, 'I see another law in my members, warring against the law of my mind, and bringing me into captivity to the law of sin which is in my members' (Rom. 7:23). It is not enough to see the use of the law in context as a written code. Rather the law is to be understood from the perspective of apocalyptic power, always seeking to re-establish the captivating power of sin over the redeemed Christian. Satan knows that sin is the only condition that can make saved souls become vulnerable to the attacks and afflictions from the kingdom of darkness. Therefore chapter 4 was an attempt to understand Paul's view of the powers and principalities in the context of spiritual warfare. His use of the language of the powers and principalities was seen more as a direct response of the kingdom of darkness, seeking to frustrate the Christian life of believers. The sole purpose of these evil forces is to ensure that believers do not run the Christian race to a successful end (2 Tim. 4:7-8).

In chapter 5, the Cross of Christ was presented as the defeat of the powers and principalities. Our primary purpose here was to look at the dethronement of Satan against the backdrop of God's redemptive and salvific work in the operations of Jesus Christ, who is the expression of God's Power, to use Paul's own language in 1 Corinthians 1:24. For Paul, Jesus Christ is the power of God, and in Him is all that believers require to fight the battle of faith. Since Christ has won complete victory for believers, they are no longer under the subjugated authority of the powers and principalities.

Chapter 6 focused on the concept of spiritual warfare in the African culture and the use of powers as a means of defence. As our reference point for the African concept of spiritual warfare, we zeroed down on the Yoruba of south-western Nigeria. In this chapter, we raised the question, 'If Paul's understanding of spiritual warfare relates to the concerted efforts a believer makes to ensure that he does not go back to the old sinful life, does spiritual warfare have the same implications in the African culture?' It is our contention that for an African, spiritual warfare is to be understood from the viewpoint of an ongoing battle against both seen and unseen powers that are not happy because of an individual's achievements. This is quite unconnected to one's level of Christian spirituality. In other words, forces of darkness do not attack primarily because a person is a Christian.

In the light of the above, for an African, spiritual warfare must be responded to promptly. Thus in chapter 6 we also looked at the various weapons for fighting spiritual battles from the African perspective. Of particular importance in this direction are the following: the practice of witchcraft, the use of magic, charms, and enlistment in the membership of secret cults. While Africans strongly believe that these are means of power to fight the many unseen battles of life, it has also been demonstrated that only the Power of God can offer genuine rescue and protection from the operations of the dark kingdom.

Chapters 7 and 8 are the climax of the study. Our aim there is to see the futility of the purported African weapons of spiritual warfare. While the fact was recognised that the many dangers of life facing the Africans had been responsible for seeking powers against the attacks of the enemies, yet, more that often, these powers had also brought them into more daunting experiences of life. It was demonstrated that rather than finding relief, more agonising experiences were the lot of mankind. But then, in such a situation, the offer of the gospel message as the Power of God has brought about total deliverance from the powers of darkness. In other words, chapter 7 clearly demonstrated that when the powers of darkness encounter the real Power of God, there is total salvation. Therefore, if there is anything that has made the Christian message a fascinating one to the Africans, it is because, in it, true deliverance has been found.

Following directly from the above is the fact that Christians need not yet seek repose, though they have been delivered from the powers of darkness; the battle is not yet over since the enemy is still seeking to draw them back to the former bondage. There is the need to be properly armed for the Christian pilgrimage. It is in this direction that chapter 8 reminds believers of the relevant weapons at their disposal for the spiritual warfare.

If a believer has been made victorious in the power of God, it certainly has a purpose, which is to be able to tell of the goodness of God. In other words, chapter 9 centred on the purpose of a God-given victory in spiritual warfare. Part of that purpose is to make known the salvation power of God to those who are still in bondage to the principalities and powers. If they commit their lives into the hands of God, and trust in Christ His Son, they too, regardless of the entanglements of the enemies, can be liberated to serve and worship God. In this chapter, we also demonstrated the fact that since Christ has overcome the powers of the dark kingdom, believers in the present age are also overcomers. This fact is being demonstrated on a regular basis in believers' involvement in deliverance and healing ministries. This is an apparent demonstration of the powerlessness of the forces of darkness when put side-by-side with the power of the living God (1 John 4:4).

As believers continue to fight the spiritual battle now in the present world, their victory is a pointer to the fact that the final doom-day for the forces of the dark kingdom is in sight. That is when believers from all tongues, all races and all languages will be ushered into the kingdom of God to worship Him eternally (Rev. 7:9-10). This is the hope of every believer who has been made victorious in the power of Christ. 'And everyone who has this hope in Him purifies himself' in expectation of the arrival of that glorious day (1 John 3:3).

In conclusion, using the words of Revelation 22:20, believers who have overcome the powers of darkness in the present ongoing spiritual warfare, having *put on* the *whole armour of God*, can joyfully say, 'Even so, come, Lord Jesus!'

References

Preface

[1]O'Brien, P.T. 'Principalities and Powers: Opponents of the Church' in *Biblical Interpretation and the Church:Text and Context*, Edited by D.A. Carson. Exeter: The Paternoster Press, 1984. p. 129.

[2]Carey, George. *Canterbury Letters to the Future*. Eastbourne, Sussex: Kingsway Publication, 1998. pp. 222-23.

[3]Macgregor, G.H.C. 'Principalities and Powers: The Cosmic Background of Paul's Thought' in *NTS I (1954)*. p. 26.

[4]I. Howard Marshall (ed.), *New Testament Interpretation: Essays on Principles and Methods*. Carlisle: Paternoster Press, 1992. p. 8.

Chapter 1

[1]Caird, G. B. *Principalities and Powers: A Study in Pauline Theology*. Oxford: The Clarendon Press, 1956. p. xi.

[2]It is important to note that there are relevant passages of the Scripture that establish each of these names. While we shall attempt to demonstrate this in what follows, suffice to say at this point that Matthew 4 well illuminates our line of thought in this direction. In 4:1, we read of 'the devil', in 4:3, we read of 'the tempter'; and in 4:10, we read of 'Satan.' All these different names refer to the same figure.

[3]Timmons, J.P. *Mysterious Secrets of the Dark Kingdom: The Battle for Planet Earth*. Austin, Texas: CCI Publishing Company, 1991. p. 71.

[4]We shall later return to this passage for our discussion of the fall of Satan. Suffice now is its use for establishing the background knowledge of the original creation and nature of Satan.

[5]For more discussion on 'cherub' (angel), see Bietenhard, H. *'angelos'* in *The New International Dictionary of New Testament Theology Volume 1: A–F*, edited by Brown. Exeter: The Paternoster Press, 1975, pages 101-103. See also Bromiley, G.W. *'Angelos'* in *Evangelical Dictionary of Theology*, edited by Walter A. Elwell. Basingstoke: Marshall Pickering, 1985, pp. 46-47.

[6]While Ezekiel 28 is very useful for the present task, it is not our intention to discuss it out of context. Further discussion is expected on this text later in this chapter.

[7]Ladd, George Eldon. *A Commentary of The Revelation of John*. Grand Rapids, Michigan: Eerdmans, 1972. p. 172.

[8]See further discussion in chapter 5 below.

[9]Calvin, John. *Calvin's Commentaries; Isaiah*. Grand Rapids, Michigan: Associated Publishers, no date. pp. 205-206.

[10]Oswalt, N. John. *The Book of Isaiah: Chapters 1-39*. Grand Rapids, Michigan: Eerdmans, 1986. p. 320.

[11]Ridderbos, J. *Isaiah: Bible Student's Commentary* (Translated by John Vriend). Grand Rapid, Michigan: Zondervan Publishing House, 1985. p. 142.

[12]Watts, D.W. John. *Isaiah 1-33: World Biblical Commentary Vol. 24*. Waxo, Texas: Word Books. 1985. p 212.

[13]Wildberger, Hans. *Isaiah 13-27: A Continental Commentary* (translated by Thomas H. Trapp). Minneapolis, MN: Fortress Press, 1997. p. 55.

[14]We have touched on this point when in our bid to establish the origin of the creation of Satan in section 1.2 above.

[15]Block, I. Daniel. *The Book of Ezekiel Chapters 25-48: The New International Commentary on the Old Testament*. Grand Rapids, Michigan: Eerdmans, 1998. p. 118.

[16]Unger, F. Merrill. *Biblical Demonology: A Study of the Spiritual Forces behind the Present World Unrest*. Wheaton, Illinois: Scripture Press, 1970. p. 15.

[17]Mounce, H. Robert. *The Book of Revelation: The New International Commentary on the New Testament*. Grand Rapids, Michigan: Eerdmans, 1977. p 240.

[18]Aune, E. David. *Revelation 6-16: Word Biblical Commentary Vol. 52B*. Nashville: Thomas Nelson Publishers, 1998. p. 695.

[19]Ladd, *A Commentary of The Revelation of John*. pp. 170-171.

[20]Although some scholars have maintained that what led to the war was the birth of a male child by the woman. Such suggestion fails to explain the outbreak of the war 'in heaven' for two reasons. First, the birth of the child was on earth by the simple fact that 'the woman fled into the wilderness' (12:6). This will be against the claim of Ladd that, 'The scene is still heaven.' (Ladd, *Revelation*, p. 170). It will be difficult to say that 'wilderness' is in heaven. Secondly, the dragon did not start 'persecuting the woman who gave birth to the male Child' (12:13) until he has been cast out of heaven with his angels. So the war had broken out, fought and won in heaven before Satan was 'cast to the earth' (12:9). Therefore, it is more plausible to see Satan's purported attempt at exalting his throne beyond that of God as the main reason for the outbreak of war in heaven.

[21]We shall be satisfied here with the working definition of 'the powers and principalities.' Chapters 4 and 5 attempt a further discussion of our understanding of the *powers and principalities* in the contexts within which they appear. In particular, chapter 5 is very helpful for understanding the New Testament concept of the powers and principalities.

[22]This conclusion is based on the role Satan played as the 'serpent of the old' in the Garden of Eden by deceiving Adam and Eve to disobey the command of God (Gen. 3:1-5). Here, Satan was seen as the opponent of

God, moving the hearts of Adam and Eve to act contrary to the divine instruction of God.

[23]O'Brien, P.T. 'Principalities and Powers: Opponents of the Church' *in Biblical Interpretation and the Church: Text and Context, Edited by D.A. Carson.* Exeter: The Paternoster Press, 1984. p. 137. (110-150).

[24]ibid. p. 146.

[25]Fape, M. Olusina. *You shall be Witnesses to Me: The Good News of Man's Restoration after the Fall.* Ibadan: Feyisetan Press, 2000. Chapter 1 of this book was devoted to addressing the subject of the uniqueness of man in God's plan of creation.

[26]Page, H.T. Sydney. *Powers of Evils: A Biblical Study of Satan and Demons.* Grand Rapids, Michigan: Baker Books, 1995. 13.

[27]Fape, *You shall be Witnesses to Me.* This issue was discussed fully in chapter 2 on pp 21-35.

[28]Carey, George. *Canterbury Letters to the Future.* Eastbourne, Sussex: Kingsway Publication, 1998. p. 222.

[29]Green, Michael. *I Believe in Satan's Downfall.* London: Hodder & Stoughton, 1988. pp. 26-27.

[30]Full discussion will be undertaken in chapter 5.

Chapter 2

[1]Fape, M. O. Paul's *Concept of Baptism and Its Present implications for Believers: Walking in Newness of Life. Toronto Studies in Theology Volume 78.* Lewiston: The Edwin Mellen Press, 1999. p. 29.

[2]ibid.

[3]We acknowledge the various scholarly debates about the authorship of Ephesians. While many scholars have argued in support of a deutero-Pauline authorship, others have thrown their weight behind the Pauline authorship. It is our aim in this work to identify with the latter. Hence Ephesians is regarded as genuinely Pauline.

[4]Lincoln, T. Andrew. *Ephesians: Word Biblical Commentary Vol. 42.* Dallas, TX: Word Books Publisher, 1990. pp. lxxv-lxxvi.

[5]Bruce, F.F. *The Epistle to the Ephesians: A Verse-by-Verse Exposition.* London: Pickering & Inglis Ltd., 1974. p. 13.

[6]Arnold, E. Clinton. *Ephesians: Power and Magic – The concept of power in Ephesians in light of its historical setting (SNTSMS 63)* (Cambridge: Cambridge University Press, 1989). In view of the transfer of dominion between the kingdoms of darkness and light, a theme that occupies a significant place in Ephesians, the use of baptism in 4:5 by the writer was to hold the new life of believers in balance. Hence after a careful survey of the importance of baptism to the new life on pages 135-136, Arnold concludes: 'This evidence does not cast doubt on the theory of the overall intention and purpose of the epistle as being a "baptismal homily" ' (p. 136).

[7]Milton, Charles Leslie. *Ephesians: New Century Bible* (London: Oliphants, 1976). The view of Goodspeed influenced the thoughts of Milton. Thus on pages 25-28, he attempted a brief survey of the interrelatedness of Ephesians to other Pauline writings and concluded: 'The one most clear and objective feature which must be accounted for is the fact that the other Pauline letters, and especially Colossians, are echoed in it [Ephesians]. It aims to present Pauline teaching in its universal and eternal aspects. This feature fits in well with the suggestion that it was written as result of a close relation to the first collection of the Pauline corpus. Its aim is to present the abiding truths of the Christian gospel as they are to be found in Paul's letter.'

[8]Lincoln, *Ephesians*, p. lxxiv.

[9]Bath, Markus *Ephesians: Introduction, Translation, and Commentary on Chapters 1-3*. New York: Doubleday & Company, 1974. p. 10.

[10]Bruce, F.F. *The Book of the Acts: The New International Commentary on the New Testament*. Grand Rapids, Michigan: Eerdmans, 1988. p. 355.

[11]Metzger, M. Bruce. 'St Paul and the Magicians.' *Princeton Seminary Bulletin 38* (1944), p. 27.

[12]Arnold, *Ephesians: Power and Magic*, p. 15.

[13]ibid.

[14]The work of Arnold is helpful in this direction. He writes: 'The primary source for our knowledge of how magic was practised during the Hellenistic era is derived from a collection of papyri discovered in the last two centuries, mainly in Egypt.' (pp 16-17). The practice of magic among the African in the contemporary society is considered in chapter six below.

[15]ibid. In chapter 6 below, when looking at magic as a weapon of spiritual warfare among the Yoruba of the South Western part of Nigeria, I shall demonstrate that the use of magic assumes the same dimension.

[16]Ibid, p. 17.

[17]Carr, Wesley. *Angels and Principalities: The background, meaning and development of the Pauline phrase, hai archai kai hai exousiai*. Cambridge: Cambridge University Press, 1981. p. 21.

[18]Barth, *Ephesians*, p. 10.

[19]It is heart warming to know that in the light of the present day scholarship, groundbreaking work has been done on the book of Acts in its first century setting, making it possible for us to know much about the city of Ephesus in the early days of the Christian faith. Noteworthy in this regard are: Winter W. Bruce and Clark D. Andrew. (Editors). *The Book of Acts in its First Century Setting Vol. 1: The Book of Acts in Its Ancient Literary Setting*. Grand Rapids: Eerdmans, 1993. Gill W.J. David and Gempf Conrad (Editors). *The Book of Acts in its First Century Setting Vol. 2: The Book of Acts in Its Graeco-Roman Setting*. Grand Rapids: Eerdmans, 1994. Rapske, B. *The Book of Acts in its First Century Setting Vol. 3: The Book of Acts and Paul in Roman Custody*. Grand Rapids: Eerdmans, 1994.

[20]The term, 'the Way,' which is used in Acts 19:23, is synonymous with the 'Christian faith'. In other words, Christians are those on 'the Way', and in this sense they are the followers of Christ, who is 'the way' (John 14:6). Therefore, the 'great commotion' that arose about 'the Way' among the Ephesians could be understood as the preaching of the good news about Jesus Christ who is 'the way, the truth, and the life' (John 14:6).

[21]Arnold, *Ephesians: Power and Magic*, p. 19. This practice is also evident among the Africans in the contemporary society. This will be demonstrated in chapter 6 below.

[22]O'Brien, T. Peter. *The Letter to the EPHESIANS: The Pillar New Testament Commentary*. Leicester: Apollos, 1999. p. 5.

[23]Arnold, Ephesians: Magic and Power, pp. 31-34.

[24]ibid, pp. 31-32.

[25]ibid.

[26]Kee, Howard Clark. *Medicine, Miracle and Magic in the New Testament Times (SNTSMS 55)*. Cambridge: Cambridge University Press, 1986. p. 107.

[27]More will be said about this later in chapter 8 where we shall discuss the believers' weapons of spiritual warfare.

[28]Hymnal Companion Hymn 356: 1

Chapter 3

[1]Caird, G. B. *Principalities and Powers: A Study in Pauline Theology*. Oxford: The Clarendon Press, 1956. From pages viii to ix, Card mentioned the relevant passages where the language of powers and principalities are used in all of Paul's Epistles with the exemption of Philemon: cf. Rom. 8:38; 1 Cor. 2:6; 2 Cor. 12:7; Gal. 4:3; Eph. 2:2; Col. 1:16; 1 Thess. 2:18. These are more obvious in the Greek Texts of the selected passages.

[2]ibid. p. x.

[3]Schlier, Heinrich. *Principalities and Powers in the New Testament*. London: Nelson, 1961. p. 13.

[4]Carr, Wesley. *Angels and Principalities: The background, meaning and development of the Pauline phrase hai archai kai hai exousiai*. Cambridge: Cambridge University Press, 1981.

[5]ibid. pp. 8, 10-24.

[6]ibid. p. 24.

[7]Charles, R.H. 'The Book of Jubilees' in *The Apocrypha and Pseudepigrapha of the Old Testament in English with Introductions and Critical and Explanatory Notes to the Several Books Vol. II*, (Edited by R.H. Charles). Oxford: The Clarendon Press, 1963.

[8]Caird, op. cit. p. 7

[9]Carr, *Angels and Principalities*, p. 24.

[10]ibid, p. 7.

[11]Arnold, *Ephesians: Power and Magic*, p. 41.

[12]Caird, *Principalities and Powers*, p. 11. I have used the transliteration of the original Greek words used in this quotation for the benefits of the readers who may not be literate in the Greek language.

[13]Macgregor, G.H.C. 'Principalities and Powers: The Cosmic Background of Paul's Thought' in *NTS I (1954)*. p. 19.

[14]ibid. p. 20.

[15]See chapter 2 for earlier discussion of Paul's ministry in Ephesus.

[16]See our discussion below on a number of interpretations in this direction.

[17]Murray, John. *The Epistle to the Romans: The English Text with Introduction, Exposition and Notes*. Grand Rapids, Michigan: Eerdmans, 1987. pp. 332-333.

[18]ibid. pp. 333-334.

[19]Carr, *Angels and Principalities*, p. 43.

[20]For a brief summary of the fact that the powers and principalities are to be understood more from the celestial point of view, see O'Brien, 'Principalities and Powers', pp. 133-136.

[21]Stewart, S. James. 'On a Neglected Emphasis in New Testament Theology' *in Scottish Journal of Theology* Vol. 4 (1951). p. 292.

[22]ibid. p. 296.

[23]O'Brien, 'Principalities and Powers', p. 117.

[24]O'Brien undertakes a brief analysis of the submissions of these scholars on pages 119 – 122 of his book: 'Principalities and Powers.'

[25]ibid. p. 119.

[26]Macgregor, 'Principalities and Powers', p. 19.

Chapter 4

[1]The issue of weapons of spiritual warfare will be considered from two angles in this study, namely the angles of unbelievers and believers (non-Christians and Christians). Both categories of humanity are engaged in spiritual warfare. However, it is our intention to focus on the weapons of spiritual warfare employed by non-Christians here, and also later in chapter 6. We shall examine the weapons of spiritual warfare available to Christians in chapter 8.

[2]The change of name from 'Saul' to 'Paul' should not constitute any problem. The two names still applied to the same and one person. Saul was the Hebrew equivalent of the Greek Paul. The change was probably effected to make him more at home with his ministry among the Gentiles, or rather the Gentiles found it more convenient to address him in their own tongue by that name.

[3]Fape, *Paul's Concept of Baptism*, p. 101. A full discussion of the on going battle in the Christian life after his conversion experience is undertaken on pages 100-105.

[4]Since this is the main text for this study, we shall defer full treatment to

chapter 8. Suffice to say here that Paul was quite aware of the fact that Christians must be ready to put up aggressive defence of their new life. There are battles to be fought, and these cannot be approached from the physical point of view. Just as the battle is spiritual, the weapons are equally spiritual.

[5]O'Brien. 'Principalities and Powers,' p. 137. So also John Stott, who sees 'principalities and powers' as being at the command of Satan. Stott, R.W. John. *The Message of Ephesians: The Bible Speaks Today*. Leicester: Inter-Varsity Press, 1979. p. 261.

[6]ibid. p. 142.

[7]This will be used interchangeably with heart. Hence there is a great flexibility in our use of the word. More importantly is that it should be seen as the thought centre of man.

[8]See our earlier discussion on the origin of powers and principalities in chapter one.

[9]This passage will receive more attention in chapter 5 below.

[10]Green, Michael. *I Believe in Satan's Downfall*. London: Hodder & Stoughton, 1988. p. 90.

[11]We shall discuss the power of the word in full as believers' weapon of warfare in chapter 8.

[12]This point has been fully discussed in chapter one.

[13]O'Brien, 'Principalities and Powers.' p. 140.

Chapter 5

[1]Green, *I Believe in Satan's Downfall*, p. 34.

[2] ibid. p 49.

[3] Niswonger, L. Richard. *New Testament History*. Grand Rapids: Zondervan Publishing House, 1992. p. 44.

[4]It is being postulated here that the same way the demonic spirits had entered into king Herod so also did Satan enter into Judas to behave strangely by betraying Christ. 'Then Satan entered Judas, surnamed Iscariot, who was numbered among the twelve' (Luke 22:3).

[5]Fee, D. Gordon. *The First Epistle to the Corinthians*. Grand Rapids, Michigan: Eerdmans, 1987. p. 105.

[6]Morris, Leon. *The First Epistle to the Corinthians: An Introduction and Commentary*. London: The Tydale Press, 1969. p. 55.

[7]Stewart, 'On a Neglected emphasis in New Testament Theology.' p.300.

[8]Apart from the text from 1 Timothy 4:1-2, Ephesians 2 as we have demonstrated in the last chapter is also instructive in this direction. For Paul writes, 'And you He made alive, who were dead in trespasses and sins, in which you once walked according to the course of this world, according to the prince of the power of the air, the spirit who now works in the sons of disobedience' (Eph. 2:1-2).

[9]Bruce, F.F. *Paul: Apostle of the Free Spirit.* Exeter: The Paternoster Press, 1977. p. 413.

[10]Macgregor, 'Principalities and Powers,' p. 22.

[11]Wright, N.T. *The Epistles of Paul to the Colossians and to Philemon: An Introduction and Commentary.* Leicester: IVP, 1986. p. 116.

[12]Bruce, *Paul: Apostle of the Free Spirit,* p. 414.

[13]Stewart, 'On a Neglected emphasis in New Testament Theology.' p.300.

[14]Bruce, F.F. *The Epistles to the Colossians, to Philemon and to the Ephesians: (NICNT).* Grand Rapids, Michigan: Eerdmans, 1984. pp. 110-112.

[15]Bruce, *The Epistles to the Colossians,* ibid. p. 110.

[16]Stewart, 'On a Neglected emphasis in New Testament Theology.' p.298.

Chapter 6

[1]Eugene Stock (ed.), *The History of the Church Missionary Society: Its Environment, its men and its, works vol. 1.* London: C.M.S., 1899. p. 449.

[2]S. O. Biobaku, *Sources of Yoruba History.* Oxford: Clarendon Press, 1973. p. 1.

[3]J. S. Eades, *The Yoruba Today.* Cambridge: Cambridge University Press, 1980. p. 4.

[4]When viewed against the backdrop of the slave trade, individuals of the Yoruba race are largely found today in sizeable proportion in different parts of the world, namely: North America, South America, Sierra Leone, the Caribbean and Cameroon. They are easily identified by their spoken language – 'Yoruba.'

[5]Daryll Forde, *The Yoruba-Speaking Peoples of South-Western Nigeria.* London: International African Institute, 1951. p. 1.

[6]Adedeji, Bunmi. *Christian Trademarks.* Ibadan: Salem Media (Nig.) Ltd., 1995. p. 78.

[7]ibid., p. 79.

[8]The Video Cassette of the Personal Testimony of Evangelist Joshua Balogun recorded at the Third Year Anniversary of the Full Gospel Businessmen Fellowship, Ijebu-Ode Chapter on Wednesday, 5th June, 1991. The testimony above was greeted by a thunderous shout of 'Praise the Lord!' The release of Evangelist Balogun from the 'iron prison' of the agents of the kingdom of darkness was a proof of the fact that indeed Christ is alive. This can be compared to Peter's experience in the book of the Acts 12:1-11.

[9]*Tell Magazine, No 10 of March 5, 2001* under the caption, 'Exploits of the Exorcist' on pages 55-57. The name used here and other names quoted from the Tell Magazine are real names.

[10]Our use of powers here is very similar to our understanding of powers in chapter 4 above.

[11]Timmons, *Mysterious Secret of the Dark Kingdom*, pp. 188-189.

[12]For a full discussion of the various wars behind the settlement of many Yoruba towns, see S.O. Biobaku, *Sources of Yoruba History* Oxford: Clarendon Press, 1973.

[13]Whenever witchcraft is mentioned, it is to be noted that wizardry is equally implied.

[14]The case of 'some of the itinerant Jewish exorcists' in Acts 19:13 can be substantiated. That they were called 'exorcists' is indicative of the fact that they had been exorcising evil spirits from demon-possessed individuals before without any counter-attack. This was a matter of stronger demonic power chasing out the weaker one. But when they wanted to do the same by using the name of Christ whom they have not confessed, they paid for it dearly (Acts 19:16). This is just a demonstration of the fact that indeed, light and darkness have nothing in common (2 Cor. 6:14).

[15]*Tell Magazine, No 10 of March 5, 2001* under the caption, 'Exploits of the Exorcist' on pages 55-57.

[16]ibid.

[17]The proposed cover design of this book is expected to reflect this understanding.

[18]This is discussed in full detail in chapter 8.

[19]Kevin-Israel, Niyi. *Understanding Dreams, Visions and Revelations.* Ibadan: Eagle Eyes Publications, 1998. pp. 13-14.

[20]A personal account of a Commission reported in the Vanguard Newspaper of Thursday, 21st June, 2001, in the Human Angle Column titled: 'Evil that women do...' The name used here in the Newspaper is not the real name of the deceased wife, just to conceal the identity of the Commissioner. *Vanguard Newspaper.* Published by Vanguard Newspaper, P.M.B. 1007, Apapa, Lagos.

[21]The Scripture bears witness to this fact. 'For everyone practising evil hates the light and does not come to the light, lest his deeds should be exposed' (John 3:20).

[22]Eni, Emmanuel. *Delivered from the Power of Darkness.* Ibadan: SU Press, 1988. On page 42-43, Emmanuel Eni, after his conversion described some of the encounters he had with the agents from the kingdom of darkness to which he previously belonged. Apart from the appearance of these agents of darkness to him in hours of night, they were also pursuing him constantly in the broad daylight. Other may not see the forces of darkness, but he did. In his own Testimony after his conversion he said, 'Other around would see me fighting with the air or see me running as if being pursued. I alone would be seeing them.'

[23]A personal account of a Commission reported in the Vanguard Newspaper of Thursday, 21st June, 2001, in the Human Angle Column titled: 'Evil that women do...' *Vanguard Newspaper.* Published by Vanguard

Newspaper, P.M.B. 1007, Apapa, Lagos.

[24]Awolalu, J. O. & Dopamu, P.A. *West African Traditional Religion.*
Ibadan: Onibonje Press and Book Industries (Nig.) Limited, 1979. pp. 244-
245.

[25]While the case being reported here happened in 1999, but for the sake
of confidentiality, names used are not the real names of the affected people.

[26]Timmons, *Mysterious Secret of the Dark Kingdom*, pp. 188-89. See the
view of Timmons expressed earlier on in connection with the efficacy of
these various articles.

[27]For instance, members of the Reformed Ogboni Fraternity pride
themselves in the fact that it was formed by a clergyman by name The Rev
TAJ Ogunbiyi, an Anglican priest. However, this is not enough justification
for its approval. After all, Satan can transform himself to an angel of light (2
Cor. 11:14).

[28]The Video Cassette of the Personal Testimony of Evangelist Joshua
Balogun recorded at the Third Year Anniversary of the Full Gospel
Businessmen Fellowship, Ijebu-Ode Chapter on Wednesday, 5th June, 1991
attests to this. Evangelist Joshua Balogun was an ardent Muslim, a staunch
member of the Reformed Ogboni Fraternity, and also belonged to many
other secret cults before he was born again. He is today involved in the
ministry of the church of God going about telling the good news of how
Jesus Christ delivered him completely from the kingdom of darkness. The
paraphernalia of these secret cults are always shown to his audience whenever
he gives his testimonies.

[29]The Testimony of Evangelist Balogun in the above Video Cassette
also confirms this claim.

Chapter 7

[1]Schlier, Heinrich. *Principalities and Powers in the New Testament.*
London: Nelson, 1961. pp. 19-20.

[2]Warneck, John. *The Living Forces of the Gospel: Experiences of a
Missionary in Animistic Heathendon.* London: Oliphant, Anderson & Ferrier,
1909. p. 189.

[3]Eni, Emmanuel. *Delivered from the Power of Darkness.* Ibadan: SU
Press, 1988. pp. 42-43.

[4]The Video Cassette of personal Testimony of Sister Sade Fadipe at the
Faith Clinic all night prayer in Ibadan on Friday, 16th December, 1989.

[5]ibid, Shade Fadipe also testified to this fact that what led her to her use
of witchcraft was the promise she received from the members that by joining
them she would be delivered from her immediate problem. However, she
found this to be empty promise after joining. It was then too late and she
could not on her own drop her membership until she met with the Lord.

[6]Warneck, *The Living Forces of the Gospel*, p. 192.

[7]Peterson, David. 'Atonement in the New Testament' in *Where Wrath & Mercy Meet: Proclaiming the Atonement Today* (ed. David Peterson). Carlisle: The Paternoster Press, 2001. p. 51.

[8]ibid. p. 53.

[9]Our usage of 'unbeliever(s)' is synonymous with 'non-Christian(s)'. So the two will be used interchangeably.

[10]The weapons of spiritual warfare at the disposal of Christians are discussed in chapter 8 below.

[11]A Report captioned 'Enter the 'Liberation Theologian' on April 5, 2001in *This Day Newspaper*, 35 Creek Road, Apapa, Lagos, Nigeria.

[12]Carey, *Canterbury Letters to the Future*, p. 165.

[13]This is quite evident in the lives of many Nigerian evangelists who were once bound by the chains of the devil, but are now freed by the power of the gospel. Few among these are Sister Sade Fadipe, Evangelist Omoba Jesus, and Evangelist Joshua Balogun. They are clear testimonies to the fact that greater is He [Jesus] who is in the believers than he [Satan] who is in the world (1 John 4:4).

[14]Warneck, *The Living Forces of the Gospel*, p. 234.

Chapter 8

[1]O'Brien, *The Letter to the Ephesians*, p. 457.

[2]Stott, R.W. John. *The Message of Ephesians: The Bible Speaks Today*. Leicester: Inter-Varsity Press, 1979. pp. 261 – 262.

[3]For a full discussion of the phrase 'put on' see Fape, *Walking in Newness of Life*, pp. 173-175.

[4]It is not our task here to attempt a full exegesis of Ephesians 6:10 –18. For a good exegesis of the text, see John Stott, *The Message of Ephesians*, pp. 260 – 287. So also, Peter O'Brien, *The Letter to the Ephesians*, p. 460 – 470. What we seek to do here is to appreciate the fact that though Christ has brought victories to believers in His death and resurrection, the battle against the emissaries of Satan is still on. This battle is not a physical one, it is spiritual, and hence requires corresponding spiritual weapons. Among the seven weapons of spiritual battle mentioned in this text by Paul, we shall exam only six. The seventh one, which is, 'the gospel of peace' will be treated in chapter 9 below as the fifth reason for being victorious over the powers of darkness.

[5]However, there is a sense in which 'righteousness' has been viewed from the objective point of view in the sense of personal growth. For instance, in the view of O'Brien, 'If the expression is to be understood in the light of its Old Testament context where righteousness is parallel to salvation, then to speak of donning God's own righteousness or appropriating his salvation is in effect to urge the readers once more to put on the 'new man' of 4:24, who is created to be like God in righteousness and holiness. By putting on

God's righteousness believers are committed to being imitators of him (5:1) and acting righteously in all their dealings.' O'Brien, *The Letter to the Ephesians*, pp. 474-475.

[6]This work recognises the debate surrounding the various 'endings of Mark.' For a review of such debates, see Hendriksen, William. *Mark: New Testament Commentary*. Edinburgh: The Banner of Truth Trust, 1975; Cranfield, C.B. *The Gospel According to Saint Mark*. Cambridge: Cambridge University Press, 1959; Lane, L. William. *The Gospel According to Mark: The English Text with Introduction, Exposition and Notes*. Grand Rapids: Eerdmans, 1988; and Mann, C.S. *Mark: A New Translation with Introduction and Commentary. The Anchor Bible, Volume 27*. Garden City, New York: Doubleday & Company, 1982. While the first two are in favour of the longer ending, the latter two are in support of the short ending. These views informed where they all ended their works on Mark respectively. However, for the purpose of this work, we accept the whole of Mark chapter 16:1-20, believing that the good news of the death and resurrection of Christ could not have ended on a gloomy note: 'And they went out quickly and fled from the tomb, for they trembled and were amazed. And they said nothing to anyone, for they were afraid' (Mark 16:8).

[7]We have discussed this in chapter 6 above.

[8]O'Brien, *Ephesians*, pp. 479-480.

[9]We have already discussed the full meaning of the word 'stronghold' in chapter four above.

Chapter 9

[1]The fact that they perceived of the power as evil is informed by the use of the phrase, 'These who have turned the world upside down.' For them, to turn 'upside down' is a destabilisation of their own existing system, which is viewed from the positive angle. Anything working contrary to this must be evil. Hence the gospel to them must be evil.

[2]Patte, Daniel. *Paul's Faith and the Power of the Gospel: A Structural Introduction to the Pauline Letters*. Philadelphia: Fortress Press, 1983. p.283.

[3]In the light of our discussion in this work, it is our contention that the principalities and powers are behind every sickness that comes upon human beings. In other words, there is a spirit behind every sickness or infirmity. The Scripture attests to this, 'And behold, there was a woman who had a spirit of infirmity eighteen years, and was bent over and could in no way raise herself up' (Luke 13:11).

[4]Chapter nine of my book, *You Shall Be Witnesses to Me*, treats this point fully. In that chapter, Christians are shown as the representatives of Christ in our world today.

[5]Ladd, George Eldon. *The New Testament and Criticism*. Grand Rapids:Eerdmans, 1991, p. 31.

[6]This is one of the seven spiritual weapons making up 'the armour of God' mentioned by Paul in Ephesians 6:14-18. This is being discussed here in view of its relevance to the present discussion.

Conclusion

[1]Coleman, Simon. *The Globalisation of Charismatic Christianity: Spreading the Gospel of Prosperity*. Cambridge: Cambridge University Press, 2000. p. 27.

[2]ibid., p. 32.

[3]Barron, Bruce. *The Health and Wealth Gospel*. Downers Grove, Illinois: IVP Press, 1987. p. 74.

AUTHORS INDEX

SUBJECT INDEX

184

Powers in Encounter with Power

SCRIPTURE INDEX

Dr. Michael Olusina Fape, an Anglican priest, received the Diploma in Theology from Immanuel College of theology, Ibadan, the Diploma in Religious Studies and BA (Hons.) from the University of Ibadan, the S.T.M. degree from Yale University Divinity School, New Haven, CT, USA, and the PhD degree from the University of Aberdeen, Scotland.

As a dedicated pastor and faithful teacher of the Word of God, Dr. Fape's pastoral and teaching ministries have brought joy to many lives in various churches in Nigeria, the USA, and Great Britain.

Dr. Fape was formerly a Senior Lecturer at Immanuel College of Theology in Ibadan, where he lectured in New Testament Studies and New Testament Greek. He is the current Dean of Archbishop Vining College of Theology, Akure, Ondo State, Nigeria. Among his other books are Paul's Concept of Baptism (Edwin Mellon Press), *Where are the Anglican Youths?* and *You Shall be Witnesses to Me*. He also has an article on Baptism in the *New Dictionary of Biblical Theology* (IVP: Leicester, UK).

He is happily married to Toyin, and they are blessed with three children: Moji, Sade and Lola.